LATIN AMERICAN DEBT IN THE 1990s

LATIN AMERICAN DEBT IN THE 1990s

Lessons from the Past and Forecasts for the Future

Edited by
Scott B. MacDonald,
Jane Hughes,
and Uwe Bott

Foreword by Norman Bailey

New York
Westport, Connecticut
London

Library of Congress Cataloging-in-Publication Data

Latin American debt in the 1990s : lessons from the past and forecasts
  for the future / edited by Scott B. MacDonald, Jane Hughes, and Uwe
  Bott.
       p.   cm.
    Includes bibliographical references and index.
    ISBN 0–275–93903–0 (alk. paper)
    1. Debts, External—Latin America.   I. MacDonald, Scott B.
II. Hughes, Jane.   III. Bott, Uwe.
HJ8514.5.L394   1991
336.3'435'098—dc20   91–2244

British Library Cataloguing in Publication Data is available.

Library of Congress Catalog Card Number: 91–2244
ISBN: 0–275–93903–0

First published in 1991

Praeger Publishers, One Madison Avenue, New York, NY 10010
An imprint of Greenwood Publishing Group, Inc.

Printed in the United States of America

(∞)™

The paper used in this book complies with the
Permanent Paper Standard issued by the National
Information Standards Organization (Z39.48–1984).

10 9 8 7 6 5 4 3 2 1

Contents

Acknowledgments

The editors wish to thank the contributors for their chapters. Scott B. MacDonald extends his appreciation to Leon Tarrant, Manager of the U.S. Interagency Country Exposure Review Committee (ICERC), at the Office of the Comptroller of the Currency, for the various ideas bounced off him and for his friendship, and Jane Hughes and Uwe Bott for being great co-editors. Others who helped stir the pot of ideas that deserve special thanks are Dr. Albert L. Gastmann at Trinity College, Dr. Fred Turner at the University of Connecticut, George Nader at *Middle East Insight*, and Sharif Ghalib at the Institute of International Finance in Washington, D.C. Above all, Scott MacDonald wishes to thank his wife, Kateri, for her patience in putting up with the long hours in front of the computer and his mother, Anita B. MacDonald, for having the stamina in raising him. Additionally, the memory of his father, Dr. Alvin R. MacDonald, helped sustain him throughout the challenges of life, especially the editing of books such as the current one.

Jane Hughes wishes to thank Scott MacDonald for his unending enthusiasm, good cheer, and good ideas throughout this process; her graduate students at Brandeis for contributing a constant stream of intellectual challenges, criticisms, and questions; her husband and children for putting up with everything; and, above all, her parents. Thanks to them, anything is possible.

Uwe Bott extends his special thanks to Leon Tarrant, Manager of the U.S. ICERC at the Office of the Comptroller of the Currency, for his helpful insights and guidance in writing the chapter on regulatory issues and to his friend, Scott MacDonald, who introduced him to the world of publishing two years ago. Above all, he wishes to thank his fiance, Celia Martens, for her patience and love.

Foreword

In the voluminous writings about the international debt crisis of the 1980s, it became commonplace to say that there was no point in trying to assign blame, because " . . . all the major players were at fault." This book tests that facile statement, which is both true and devoid of significance, because it is precisely about the role in the ongoing crisis of all the major actors. It is simply not good enough to say this when referring to a situation that put the entire financial structure of the Western world at risk and that has measurably and demonstrably raised the quantum of human misery in this last quarter of the twentieth century in precisely those parts of the world least able to bear it.

There is no doubt whatsoever that the world would be better off and a better place if the tidal wave of international commercial balance of payments lending had not taken place. Even those institutions and individuals who appeared for a time to be benefiting greatly have, in the majority of cases, fallen victim to their own stupidity and greed.

That being the case, it is by no means obvious that blame should not be assigned, not for the purposes of retribution—others are taking care of that— but for the wholly constructive reason of drawing lessons that may help to avoid similar events in the future, although financial history gives little hope in this regard.

In the first chapter, Scott MacDonald, Jane Hughes, and Uwe Bott set forth a number of lessons that might profitably be learned. I subscribe to them all. In summary forms (as appropriate to a foreword) and in no particular order, I offer five more:

Sloppy, intermittent, and episodic banking regulation's are worse than none at all.

A financial institution has a fiduciary responsibility to its depositors. This responsibility is more important than its responsibility to its shareholders and much more important than its responsibility to its officers.

The possibility of institutional failure is just as vital to financial capitalism as it is to commercial, industrial, or personal capitalism.

The timidty of international business is truly remarkable. It cannot be trusted to defend its own interests.

The international financial institutions should stick to their assigned functions: the International Monetary Fund to provide liquidity relief where appropriate; the World Bank and the regional development banks to finance physical and social infrastructure, the International Finance Corporation and similar institutions to finance private productive activities. There is no institution to provide insolvency relief, nor should there be.

This is a good book. More important, it is a useful one. If all the lessons contained in it are learned, the world will be improved substantially. If not, and the smart money has to be on this alternative, we are fated to repeat the old story of financial boom and crash at least one more time.

Norman A. Bailey, Ph.D.
Consulting Economist
Formerly Special Assistant
to the President (Reagan)
for International Economic Affairs

LATIN AMERICAN DEBT IN THE 1990s

1   # Latin America in the 1990s: Democracy in Debt?

Scott B. MacDonald,* Jane Hughes, and Uwe Bott

INTRODUCTION

In the 1980s, Latin America was swept by two waves: one political and the other economic and financial. The first was "democratic revolution," which brought with it a sense of euphoria and hope for the future. The latter was the debt crisis, which brought in most cases a sense of gloom and frustration. It is the purpose of this book to examine the interrelationship between the external debt problem and the consolidation of democracy in Latin America in the 1990s. The book considers the interplay of actors and environment in the new decade, focusing on whether or not Latin America's political regimes can strengthen and democratize their respective economies while continuing to guarantee the country's democratic politics. In this context, the foreign debt problem casts a long shadow.

Democratic governments in Latin America in the 1990s are confronted with a myriad of economic problems, ranging from hyperinflation and capital flight to the constriction of the gross domestic product (GDP) and eroding infrastructures. The human dimension is often reflected by closed factories, falling health and educational standards, and rising levels of drug abuse. The economic reforms that many Latin American countries have implemented and are in the process of implementing we hope will create stronger, more diversified economies capable of providing an improved standard of living. This is, however, a long-term

*Scott B. MacDonald is an official of the Office of the Comptroller of the Currency (OCC). The views expressed here do not represent the OCC in any fashion and are solely those of the authors.

hope. In the meantime, the way forward is painful, occasionally disorienting, and often politically distasteful.

Riots in Argentina and Venezuela in 1989 indicate that tensions exist beneath the surface and that Latin America is at another crossroads in its development. One direction offers the consolidation of democracy and economic recovery. Other directions are potentially nondemocratic and economically disastrous or more of the same—a gradual incremental crisis in development in which the region as a whole becomes less competitive in the international system. At the same time, it should be emphasized that the comments here are broad generalizations. It is understood that each country is unique in its external debt management as well as path of democratization.

LESSONS FROM THE DEBT CRISIS

The debt for Latin America commenced in August 1982 with the "Mexican Weekend," when Mexico informed its creditors and the U.S. government of its inability to pay its debt.[1] Since that event, there have been numerous reschedulings, stabilization, and structural adjustment programs and riots. The debt problem has become an almost standard electoral issue and, on occasion, it has been an awkward foreign policy issue between the industrialized nations and Latin America. It has also complicated relations between Latin American countries as in the case of Argentina's debt with Bolivia and Paraguay's or Suriname's debt with Brazil.

There has been a considerable sea of ink spilt discussing the hows and whys of the debt crisis and this book will not venture along that well-tread path.[2] However, six lessons were learned about the impact of the debt crisis on Latin America, which should prove valuable in assessing prospects for political regime change and democratic consolidation in the 1990s.

The first lesson is that by the end of the 1980s, the debt crisis has stretched out into a chronic debt problem. In the early and mid-1980s, there was a sense of impending doom related to this issue as well as a perceived threat to the international financial system. However, as the "crisis" has continued for certain actors in the drama and not for others and has gone on into the next decade, is it still a "crisis"? The nature of the beast has changed: the debt problem is likely to be long-term and structural as opposed to initial perceptions that it was simply a short-term liquidity crunch.

The second lesson is that the debt issue has become politicized. As Joan Nelson noted, stabilization aimed at reducing balance of payments deficits and inflation to levels compatible with resumed and sustainable growth and structural change "designed to encourage foreign exchange earning or savings activities and, more generally, to improve incentives and efficiency for sustainable growth," have "provoked intense controversy."[3]

That controversy rages between monetarists and structuralist economists as well as between politicians favoring "orthodox" economic policies and populists who regard stabilization and structural adjustment with outright suspicion. This debate has had clear repercussions in the region's politics, while the effects of such policies have been shocks to daily life for the vast majority of Latin Americans. In a sense, the political impact of the debt problem and strategies to resolve it have launched the region into a quest for a new consensus on how to approach development in the future. With this quest comes the question about Latin America's role in a changing world. Political and economic interest groups in each country have lined up in the development issue with different outcomes. Along these lines, Nelson commented: "Why have structural reforms failed to get off the ground in some countries and forged ahead in others? And why, when confronted with heated political protest, have some governments persisted, while others have modified or abandoned their courses? The answers to these questions are mainly political, not economic."[4]

The third lesson concerns who is more affected by the debt problem. In many regards, Latin American indebtedness has receded as a crisis for most commercial banks in North America, Europe, and Japan. Most banks have put up substantial reserves against bad loans and a number, especially U.S. regional banks and some large Canadian banks, have sold large amounts of their troubled assets in the secondary market.[5]

Although troubled Latin American debt remained a problem for those banks that have kept it, the immediate danger to the global financial network receded in the late 1980s. By February 27, 1989, *The Economist* could credibly write about "the banks' great escape," and the May 1989 issue of the trade journal *Latin Finance* was announcing retrospectively that "1990 was the year that the major banks declared the debt crisis over."[6]

There was no great escape for the majority of Latin American countries. For all the austerity and adjustment programs and good intentions, few Latin American countries in the 1982–1989 period achieved substantial debt reduction. Table 1.1 demonstrates this.

The fourth lesson is that the debt problem has carried in its wake falling per-capita incomes, reductions in social services and a marked erosion of health standards. The 1980s have consequently been called the "lost decade," which will be remembered as a time of adjustment and austerity as well as a period in which countries devoured their own infrastructures.

Although the data on health care in Latin America vary considerably country by country, making comparisons difficult, in 1984, the Pan American Health Organization reported that "many countries face sharp increases in the prevalence of malaria. Mortality due to infectious diseases and malnutrition is increasing."[7] In fact, in 1984, 188,851 blood samples taken in Central America proved positive for malaria, twice as many as ten years earlier. Central America is not the only region within Latin America affected: in 1989 and 1990, there was a serious outbreak of dengue fever in Venezuela and yellow fever had returned to several urban areas in Brazil.

Latin America has another health problem that was carried into the 1990s.

Table 1.1
Selected Latin American Debtors (in U.S. $ billions)

	1982	1989a
Argentina	43.6	61.9
Bolivia	3.3	5.8
Brazil	92.2	112.7
Chile	17.3	18.5
Colombia	10.3	18.2
Ecuador	7.9	11.5
Mexico	86.0	102.6
Uruguay	2.7	4.5
Venezuela	32.0	34.1
Total	$307.6	$389.7

a. estimates

Source: The World Bank, *World Debt Tables, 1989–90, Vol. 2, Country Tables* (Washington, D.C.: The World Bank, 1989).

Drug abuse is becoming a problem in a number of societies. In 1987, Colombian health sources revealed that 600,000 Colombians were reported to have serious drug problems, of which an estimated 400,000 were *basuco* smokers.[8] In 1989, Argentina reported 100,000 cases of addiction to one substance or another (mainly cocaine). Bolivia, Chile, and Venezuela also report increasing problems with drug abuse.

The debt problem is increasingly more of a Latin concern than a North American and European concern. In terms of health care and infrastructure development, it has meant reduced funds and a return to old problems, such as disease control. Moreover, the debt problem has its place in the inter-American illicit drug trade. As one study noted of the interrelationship: ''The Latin debt crisis cannot be blamed as the cause of the drug trade in the Americas, but it is part of the problems. Austerity programs often deplete law enforcement budgets, reduce already low salaries, and drive down the nation's standard of living. These conditions, in turn, create a lack of resources for launching and sustaining effective antinarcotics campaigns and thus open the door to official corruption.''[9]

The fifth lesson is that the prolonged nature of the debt problem has led to a differentiation between countries in Latin America.[10] There are now blatant and growing differences between those that have been more successful in implementing economic reforms and returning in some form to international capital markets and those countries that continue to have massive problems.

Politics aside, Chile and Mexico have been more successful than most Latin American countries in controlling inflation, diversifying products and markets, and external debt management (especially after Mexico signed a Brady Plan debt reduction accord). Chile was the first to successfully complete a Brady Plan debt buyback, accepting $139.8 million worth of debt buyback at an average discount price of 58.25 cents on the dollar.[11] In 1989, Chile's economic growth was a brisk 9.9 percent. Although inflation rose from 12.7 percent in 1988 to 21.4 percent, it was one of the lowest throughout Latin America.[12]

Chile also represents a rare case of net debt reduction in Latin America. Although total external debt has not fallen below 1982's $17.3 billion, the country's debt-equity conversion program has been an effective mechanism in retiring $6.2 billion between 1984 and 1988.[13] Chile's foreign debt peaked in 1987 at $21.5 billion. Through export-led growth, debt-equity conversion, and positive currency changes, external debt fell in 1988 to $19.6 billion and to an estimated $18.5 billion in 1989.[14]

Mexico's external debt has also fallen from a high of $109.2 billion in 1987 to an estimated $102.6 billion in 1989.[15] On other fronts, Mexico's inflation rate in 1989 was the lowest for that country in 10 years, having fallen from a high of 159 percent in 1987 to 19.7 percent.[16] Moreover, the growth rate was around 3 percent. As Abraham Lowenthal commented in 1990: "Mexico, in particular seems embarked on a course of policy that, if sustained over time, may make it increasingly a North American nation, ever more different and removed from Latin America."[17]

Other relatively successful countries have been Colombia, Costa Rica, and Uruguay. Venezuela also has the potential to be highly successful as it is undergoing a painful, yet far-reaching structural adjustment of its economy. The same can be said of Colombia. The government of President César Gaviria, which came to office in 1990, is representative of a new generation that wishes to modernize the economy, to make it more efficient and responsive to the population through liberalization of the trading regime, to stimulate the stock market (*bolsa*), and to open the economy to outside competition. Gaviria's intention to privatize the national telephone company is a clear signal of the direction his government has taken.

In contrast, Argentina, Brazil, and Peru entered the 1990s carrying the unwanted baggage of hyperinflation and economic stagnation. Argentina's monthly inflation rate in December 1989 was 40.1 percent, or 4,923 percent on an annual basis. Peru's year-end inflation in 1989 was 2,775 percent and Brazil's was over 4,500 in the year to March 1990. Peru's situation continued to unravel as inflation, in August 1990, went over the 3,000 percent mark on an annual basis and reached triple digits for monthly inflation.

The problems of these three countries in particular cannot be entirely blamed on the debt problem: Argentina did not pay on its commercial bank debt from April 1988 to July 1990, when it began to pay a symbolic $50 million a month; Brazil has not paid its commercial banks since July 1989; and Peru has been problematic throughout the decade. Part of the problem rests in adverse international conditions: fluctuating commodity prices and interest rates and protectionism in industrialized country markets. And part of the problem has been economic mismanagement, corruption, and the failure of the import substitution model as a viable strategy for overcoming dependency. Furthermore, the dangerous buildup in arrearages, around $7 billion for Argentina (mid–1990), makes the restoration of relations with international creditors more difficult.

Cuba is another country that is deeply troubled economically and runs the risk of falling behind in the development game. Entering the 1990s with a large external debt, strained relations with the Soviets, and a breakdown in ties to many East European countries, the Castro government is also isolated from the rest of the Americas that have opted for the democratic path. Cuba runs the risk of becoming one of the most fossilized "Communist" states, with the potential that even Albania may become more democratized and economically open at a faster rate in the 1990s.

In addition to Cuba and the troubled South American countries, most nations in Central America and in the Caribbean are facing difficult periods of economic stress. Political turmoil in El Salvador and Surinam preclude serious efforts to reform the economy, and Honduras, Guyana, and Panama struggle to implement structural adjustment programs while coming to grips with large debt burdens. The situation is not helped by the already low level in the standard of living and the potential that it will fall further before it improves.

The sixth lesson concerns regime change and the ability or inability of democratic and authoritarian governments to deal with economic problems. This lesson is closely related to the second lesson—concerning the politicalization of the debt problem. As Robert Kaufman and Barbara Stallings noted: "In the 1960s and 1970s, as democracies in the region were shaken by political immobilism and severe stagflation crises, much of the conventional wisdom held that it was especially difficult for governments to manage economies in the context of competitive elections, populist politics, and interest group pluralism. Subsequent comparative studies, however, have suggested that for much of the post-war period the macroeconomic performance of authoritarian regimes has not been any better."[18] Chile, however, may provide an example of successful economic management by an authoritarian regime. At the same time, the democratically elected Aylwin government over time might demonstrate the opposite.

An important element concerning regime type and survival may be the approach adopted to economic crisis. Those governments that have used a narrow approach to economic crisis via stabilization, without a longer term approach to structural adjustment have not been overly successful, politically or economically. An example of this failure to adopt long-term strategies in a democratic setting is the Dominican Republic. As Nelson wrote: "The initial Dominican effort, abrupt and ill-prepared, ignited a political explosion in April 1984. A more carefully prepared austerity program later in 1984 and 1985 succeeded in temporarily restoring economic balance and growth. But the program remained an isolated episode, followed neither by structural change nor disciplined economic management."[19]

In both the Mexican and Chilean cases, de la Madrid in the former and Pinochet in the latter, stabilization was used first as a precursor to a longer-term process. In one of the region's longest running democracies, however, the Venezuelans appear to be accomplishing the same thing. In other democracies like Argentina, Brazil and Peru, the effort is being made, but the ability of those governments to carry through anything beyond stabilization is questionable.

REFLECTIONS OF LATIN ATTITUDES ABOUT DEBT: BRAZIL AND PERU

The Brazilian elections for the presidency in November and December 1989 provide some insight as to attitudes vis-à-vis foreign debt. Although Brazil does not represent all of Latin America, it is the world's largest developing country debtor with an estimated $112.7 billion foreign debt in 1989. It also underwent the transition from an authoritarian regime at the beginning of the decade to the stage of direct presidential elections in 1989. Furthermore, the country is significant in terms of size: despite substantial economic problems, Brazil is the ninth largest economy in the world.

In August 1989, prior to the first round of presidential voting, a poll was conducted by a Brazilian firm (IBOPE), which surveyed 2,663 voters in five regions. It was significant that although inflation was regarded by 53 percent of those polled as the country's major problem, 38 percent felt that the foreign debt was first. Other concerns were unemployment, government corruption, and government incompetence.

The next question was even more direct in terms of what to do with the external debt, asking what position the new president should take in dealing with foreign bankers. Significantly, 24 percent felt that Brazil should continue paying in the same amounts; 31 percent that they should continue paying, but in smaller amounts; 11 percent that they should stop paying now and pay later; and only 20 percent favored not paying at all. Fifteen percent did not know. Surprisingly, a clear-cut majority of 66 percent favored debt repayment, although by varying formulas.

Another interesting finding was the response when people were asked to choose between capitalism, socialism, and communism. The pollings revealed that 39 percent favored socialism, 29 percent capitalism, only 7 percent communism, and 25 percent did not know. Although socialism drew the most favorable response, the word had a different meaning in the Brazilian context when compared to North American and European perceptions. Many Brazilians regard socialism as a desire to place more emphasis on social needs. Moreover, there is an overlap with "populism." In other IBOPE surveys, populism usually received the highest approval rating and was observed as "democratic and egalitarian."

Another possible reason for the high rating of socialism is the deep socioeconomic divisions and poverty in Brazil. An additional factor is that Brazil is traditionally a patrimonial society in which the state has played a substantial role in the economy.

Although this survey of Brazil should not be overstated and the representation of that country should not be overblown with regard to the rest of the region, two major points can be drawn from it with regard to how Latin America faces the challenges of the 1990s. First and foremost, a majority of Brazilians occupy a middle ground that favors either socialism or capitalism or some combination of the two—like European-style social democracy. Second, there is an interest in coming to terms with the problem of paying foreign debt, but little consensus on how. To these two points should be added a third: other surveys have demonstrated that Brazilians tend to prefer democracy to other forms of government.

Survey research conducted by Apoyo, S.A., in Peru in 1989 reflected some of the same attitudes about external debt.[20] In terms of identifying the country's major economic problem, 57 percent of Peruvians polled regarded inflation as the most significant, with 15 percent feeling the same about unemployment. External debt was fourth with 8 percent thinking it was the country's major economic problem. Another question asked whether or not the external debt should be paid.[21] Although 83 percent felt that the debt should be repaid, 74 percent did not feel that the country had the means to pay.

Apoyo provided another interesting question regarding preference of system of government. This question was asked in 1987, 1988, and 1989. Although a clear majority favored democracy, the percentage declined from a high of 86 percent in 1987 to 61 percent in 1989. At the same time, the preferences for other systems of government increased: preference for a military regime grew from 6 to 14 percent and preference for a revolution grew from 5 to 8 percent, both over the 1987–1989 period. Those that were undecided also grew from 5 to 17 percent, reflecting increasing dissatisfaction with the political system. Although the debt problem should not be overstated as a cause, it has played a role in the country's overall economic crisis that has in many respects undermined support for the democratic system.

CHALLENGES IN THE 1990s
TO THE CONSOLIDATION OF DEMOCRACY

Although democracy has been restored throughout most of Latin America, there are considerable questions about its ability to deal with the complexities of problems now confronting the region's societies.[22] One school of thought is relatively negative and argues that democracy in Latin America functions poorly. As an editorial in *The Financial Times* noted:

Constitutions are ill-adapted to deal with the complexities of modern government or political pluralism. Political parties are drifting in an increasingly nonideological environment, in which the bulk of the electorate occupies a social democratic middle ground. The traditional party politician is seen as self-seeking, corrupt and remote, encouraging the rise of a new type of candidate, especially in presidential elections, with a non-party and clean government appeal. This may produce popular leaders, but they are handicapped by having to deal with legislative bodies in the hands of parties they do not control.[23]

There are two points of departure from the *Financial Times'* assessment. Many Latin Americans are willing to try democracy after long years of authoritarian government (reflected in survey research) and democracies in many cases came to power during a period of economic crisis that led to the demise of an authoritarian regime. Furthermore, the newly restored democracies, as in Argentina and Peru, have (to date) demonstrated an amazing resilience in the face of tough challenges: popular discontent with austerity measures in the form of riots and strikes and even attempted military coups (as in Argentine case).

There are two major dangers to consider for the 1990s with regard to the relationship between debt and democracy in Latin America. Both major dangers for democratic governments raise the threat of debt fatigue that can be compounded by "political fatigue" caused by the inability of elected leaders and their parties to cooperate in resolving parliamentary stalemates over pressing economic issues. The threat is the loss of legitimacy for the government and the democratic system. A case in point is Argentina, where public opinion polls have indicated that because of the country's ongoing economic crisis, both major parties have become discredited in the eyes of the people.[24]

Latin American countries run the risk of becoming economically irrelevant in the international economic system due to the external debt problem and local economic systems not capable of competing. On an overall regional basis, the threat is that Latin America as an economic whole becomes irrelevant in the international system. Latin America's significance in the 1980–1987 period, according to World Bank data, has already slipped as demonstrated in the region's percentage of global GDP from 13.6 percent in 1980 to around 4.8 percent in 1987.[25] Another estimate put the decline from around 4 percent in 1982 to around 2 percent in 1988.[26] With the substantial economic changes occurring in Eastern Europe and the Middle East and the rise of East Asia's Newly Industrializing Economies (NIEs), Latin America as a region has entered the last decade of the twentieth century with a substantial debt overhang and declining competitiveness. Moreover, with Japan and the Pacific Rim increasingly taking over a position of leadership in world financial circles, the danger of marginalization grows for Latin America.

The second danger is that of economic differentiation. As the more successful countries leave behind the less successful countries, it will be more difficult to form regional common markets that can support democracy as well as joint marketing efforts as in the European Community. The development of regional common markets (or, at the very least, freer trade) would also provide greater strength for many Latin American countries in the global economy. The combination of growing economic irrelevance and economic differentiation carries the threat of being left out of a world of emerging trade blocs. These trading blocs include the European Community, the Free Trade Agreement between Canada and the United States, and the Association for Southeast Asian Nations. As Marcus Vinicius de Morães, head of the Brazilian Export Association, commented: "Where does a struggling Latin America fit into this scenario?"[27]

The way forward for Latin America in the 1990s is likely to be difficult. The consolidation of democracy is not a given, but a development that will have to fought for. As Mac Margolis noted of Brazil in early 1990: "The overhauling is a tumultuous, painful process, replete with fingerpointing and caustic debate. But out of it may come the scaffolding for building society anew, the formula for reinventing Brazil."[28] Even in Chile, often regarded as one of the region's success stories, the Aylwin government has been forced to debate important questions concerning the balance between economic growth and social equalities.

Latin American countries will have to continue painful economic adjustment if they are going to return to international competitiveness as well as reach an agreement with their creditors about what to do with the external debt. New funds are needed for the modernization of an aging industrial infrastructure and the upgrading of educational systems required for the next waves of change in the global economy. International cooperation is important, especially through the World Bank, the International Monetary Fund, the Caribbean Development Bank, and the Inter-American Development Bank. The Brady Plan also holds out the promise that if local reforms are carried out by each country, a framework for international cooperation exists for the purpose of debt reduction. Moreover, regional cooperation is critical, especially in the development of free-trade agreements needed to enhance Latin American exports and compete with the rise of trade blocs elsewhere.

There is the possibility of a slide backwards to authoritarian regimes as democratic systems fail in their promises to deliver more egalitarian societies and cut the Gordian Knot of external debt. As the 1960s and 1970s marked the rise of dictatorships and the 1980s of democracies, the 1990s could mark a return to authoritarian governments. Some observers already note a return of "creeping authoritarianism" in Argentina and Brazil. There is also the possibility that the economic differentiation process will continue to make itself felt in the region, creating two, perhaps three, Latin Americas based on economic and political development. Strong democracies such as Chile, Colombia, Costa Rica, and Venezuela could lead the way over fragile democracies, plagued by severe economic crises, as in the Argentine and Peruvian cases.

CONCLUSION

The Latin American experience is important to understand, especially in the light of changes in Eastern Europe. Despite the obvious cultural differences and historical experiences, there are many parallels between the two regions—democratization at a time of economic crisis and, with the exception of Romania, of heavy external debt as well. As in the case of Latin America, the euphoria that came from the termination of authoritarian regimes, however, could rapidly disappear in the face of economic realities. There are many difficult questions to be confronted: How to make economies work? How to put people to work? How to deal with foreign debt? The answers, as many Latin American countries have already experienced, are difficult and are not entirely dependent on outside forces: for example, Eastern European economies were jolted by the 1990 Persian Gulf crisis, which pushed oil prices up, while the Soviet decision to sell its oil to the West for hard currency instead of barter with Eastern Europe was equally disruptive.

Both Latin America and Eastern Europe face a new decade of change and the establishment of political order within a democratic context will be difficult. Furthermore, it takes time and experimentation to fully comprehend that the democratization process also includes economic reform. The restructuring of the Chilean, Mexican, and Venezuelan economies, a process that is ongoing, offers a better foundation for democracy and a successful solution to the debt problem than the failed economic experiments of import substitution as in Argentina and Peru. In both Latin America and Eastern Europe, the desire for meaningful change toward political and economic democracy will have to come from within—otherwise regime legitimacy will remain a mirage and outside cooperation will mean little.

Thus, in order to assess the prospects for the 1990s, this book examines the actors and environment affecting the Latin American debt issue. Actors include creditor governments, international financial institutions, debtor country actors, and commercial banks. Analysis of the environment focuses on social conditions, regulatory aspects, and world economic conditions. The interplay of these actors with this environment will, in turn, determine whether or not the 1990s will be another lost decade in Latin America.

NOTES

1. Other Latin American countries were forced to reschedule before the Mexican weekend in August 1982. Jamaica rescheduled in 1979 and Bolivia, Nicaragua, and Peru in 1980. What made the debt crisis "begin" in 1982, however, was the magnitude of Mexico's external debt. Furthermore, other major debtors like Argentina and Brazil were soon following Mexico into the crisis. For further information, see World Bank, *World Debt Tables, 1989–90* (Washington, D.C.: World Bank, December 1989).

2. The literature on the Latin American debt crisis is extensive and the following is meant to be a small menu. Joan M. Nelson, editor, *Economic Crisis and Policy Choice: The Politics of Adjustment in the Third World* (Princeton: Princeton University Press, 1990); William Guttman, *Between Bailout and Breakdown: A Modular Approach to Latin America's Debt Crisis* (Washington, D.C.: The Center for Strategic and International Studies, 1989); Barbara Stallings, *Banker to the Third World: U.S. Portfolio Investment in Latin America, 1900–1986* (Berkeley: The University of California Press, 1987); Pedro-Pablo Kuczynski, *Latin American Debt* (Baltimore: The Johns Hopkins University Press, 1988); and Felipe Ortiz de Zevallos, *The Peruvian Puzzle* (New York: Priority Press, 1989).

3. Joan M. Nelson, "Introduction: The Politics of Economic Adjustment in Developing Nations," in Joan M. Nelson, editor, *Economic Crisis and Policy Choice*, pp. 3–4.

4. Ibid., p. 4.

5. The secondary market is the market in which developing country debt, usually troubled debt, is bought and sold as an asset, usually at a discount. The market functions on the concept that such debt is not worth the face value, hence the discount price. Secondary market activities include debt swaps, debt-for-equity conversions, and debt-for-nature swaps.

6. Quoted from Michael Hobbs, "Debt Policies for an Evolving Crisis," in Scott B. MacDonald, Margie Lindsay, and David L. Crum, editors, *The Global Debt Crisis: Forecasting for the Future* (London: Pinter Publishers, 1990).

7. Pan American Health Organization, *Priority Needs in Central America and Panama* (Washington, D.C.: Pan American Health Organization, November 1984), p. 27.

8. Quoted in Richard D. Craig, "Illicit Drug Traffic: Implications for South American Source Countries," *Journal of Interamerican Studies and World Affairs*, Vol. 29, No. 2 (Summer 1987), p. 24.

9. Scott B. MacDonald, *Mountain High, White Avalanche: Cocaine and Power in the Andean States and Panama* (New York: Washington Papers of the Center for Strategic and International Studies/Praeger Publishers, 1989), p. 134.

10. See Abraham F. Lowenthal, "Latin America Enters the 1990s," *The Aspen Institute Quarterly*, Vol. 2, No. 3 (Summer 1990), pp. 57–60.

11. "Chile Ends Brady Buyback, Bidders Get Second Chance," *LDC Debt Report*, November 27, 1989, p. 1.

12. Barbara Durr, "Chile's Growth Rises to 9.9%," *The Financial Times*, January 10, 1990, p. 6.

13. Roberto Tosso, Financial Representative of the Banco de Chile, during the Debt Conversion Workshop held on February 9, 10, and 11, 1989, Abidjan, Cote d'Ivorie, speech entitled "Debt Conversion Programs in Chile," p. 8.

14. World Bank, *World Debt Tables 1989–90, Vol. 2, Country Tables*, p. 70.

15. Ibid., p. 254.

16. Richard Johns, "Mexico Inflation at 10-Year low," *The Financial Times*, January 10, 1990, p. 6. Also see Banamex, *Review of the Economic Situation of Mexico* (Mexico City), November 1989.

17. Lowenthal, "Latin American Enters the 1990s," p. 58.

18. Robert Kaufman and Barbara Stallings, "Debt and Democracy in the 1980s: The Latin American Experience," in Barbara Stallings and Robert Kaufman, editors, *Debt and Democracy in Latin America* (Boulder, Colorado: Westview Press, 1989), p. 201.

19. Joan M. Nelson, "The Politics of Adjustment in Small Democracies: Costa Rica, the Dominican Republic, Jamaica," in Joan M. Nelson, editor, *Economic Crisis and Policy Choice*, p. 170.

20. Alfredo Torres Gúzman, *Perfil del elector* (Lima: Editorial Apoyo, 1989).

21. Ibid., p. 102.

22. The most evident exceptions are Cuba and Guyana, although some observers would include Mexico and Surinam in this category.

23. "Latin America's Next Decade," *The Financial Times*, December 29, 1989, p. 10.

24. See Edgardo Catterberg, "Las dos elecciones presidenciales y la transición argentina a la democracia," paper presented at the World Association for Public Opinion Research conference on the Consolidation of Democracy in Latin America, Caracas, Venezuela, January 16, 1990.

25. This figure was estimated by the authors from data extracted from the World Bank, *World Bank Development Report 1982* (New York: Oxford University Press, 1982), p. 114; and the World Bank, *World Bank Development Report 1989* (New York: Oxford University Press, 1989), p. 168. World Bank data did not include the Soviet Union, Bulgaria, East Germany, Vietnam, Mongolia, and Albania. By including the Soviet Union in the world GDP in 1987, Latin America's share falls from 4.8 percent to 4.1 percent.

26. This figure was advanced by Steve Daichi at a presentation on Brazil at the Center for Strategic and International Studies in Washington, D.C., on December 21, 1989.

27. Quoted in Mac Margolis, "Brazil's Bad Dreams," *Best of Business Quarterly*, Spring 1990, p. 72.

28. Ibid.

2 Actors in the Latin American Debt Crisis I: The Creditor Governments

Jane Hughes

INTRODUCTION

Creditor governments are key players in the Latin American debt game, affecting developments in numerous ways. Most obviously, governments are creditors themselves, through the provision of trade finance and development aid in particular. As will be discussed in this chapter, however, the bulk of Latin debt is owed to commercial banks rather than governments. Governments also play an important role as regulators of their own domestic banking systems, which, in turn, affect banks' flexibility in the negotiating process. Bank regulators have a great deal of leeway in determining at what point, and to what degree, commercial banks must write down the value of Latin American credits. This then helps determine what position the banks will take in negotiating a deal with debtor nations. Perhaps the most important role of creditor governments, however, is the most subtle one: that of power broker and kingmaker behind the scenes, rather than as a direct participant in the process. Governments are actively exercising their moral suasion rights in various ways throughout the debt negotiation process. Intense pressure may be exerted by a government on its commercial banks or the International Monetary Fund to take an accommodating stance in debt talks—as the United States does for Mexico and the Philippines, for example—or governments may stand aloof from the process, implying disapproval or distaste for a debtor nation (Argentina, for instance). This will in turn have a strong, if unspoken, influence on bankers' willingness to show leniency toward a recalcitrant debtor.

The topic of creditor governments subsumes a vast array of different players, each representing an equally vast array of different interests. Obviously, each individual government focuses on its own set of priorities and concerns. Strategic and diplomatic interests, for example, will vary widely from country to country. Thus, U.S. economic policy toward countries such as Egypt and Israel is deeply colored by its geopolitical interests there, as is West European policy toward the former Eastern bloc nations. Similarly, each government's economic and financial interest in a debtor nation, based on its trade and investment ties as well as commercial bank exposure, will also influence its stance on the debt issue; examples here range from the U.S. economic interest in Mexico to Japan's ties with Indonesia. This broad range of interests will, in turn, dictate the government's attitude when one of these countries encounters problems servicing its foreign debt. Case studies of early debt crises during the 1970s suggest that countries of strategic importance such as Egypt or great potential wealth such as Indonesia won heavy involvement by Western governments when debt problems arose, helping to bring matters to a successful and speedy conclusion. This left open, of course, the question of what would happen if a country like Argentina got into trouble; its geopolitical importance to the United States is not on the same level as that of Mexico or Egypt, and its potential wealth is not as easily tapped or near-term as Indonesia's.[1]

Although it is clear that each creditor government has its own agenda to pursue, it is less clear that within each government is another host of differing players with differing interests. These parties range from the central bank to congressmen, and the proliferation of constituencies represented by these groups further complicates the formulation of debt policy. The central bank, for example, is responsible for maintaining financial stability, ensuring that domestic banks are sound, and supporting a healthy international financial system. Elected officials (e.g., congressmen, members of parliament, presidents, prime ministers) may represent sectors that demand protection against foreign imports and fiercely oppose taxpayer bailouts of commercial banks or developing countries. The U.S. Congress, for example, was strongly supporting trade sanctions against Brazil at the same time that the Federal Reserve Board and the Treasury Department were laboring mightily to create a debt package that rested heavily on the achievement of a sizeable current account surplus. The foreign policy establishment is most concerned with political stability, until recently focusing in the United States on the fight against communism and the growing strength of leftists in Latin America. Finally, trade officials aim to increase trade with developing nations by cutting trade barriers and providing export credit. It is clear that while conflict is going on between creditor governments on how to deal with the debt crisis, another set of conflicts is ongoing within each government itself on the very same topic.

This explains why Western government treatment of Latin American debtors has been uneven, frequently confused, and sometimes even contradictory. However, it is becoming clear that two emerging issues will dominate the topic of creditor government relations with Latin America over the next decade. First of all, developments in Eastern Europe will undoubtedly distract both funds and attention from Latin America throughout the 1990s. The question is whether or not this will occur, but to what extent it will occur. Will Latin America get an adequate share of Western government involvement, or will the industrialized world remain obsessed with events in Eastern Europe?

Second, shifting power blocs within the Western alliance will be of increasing concern to Latin America. Declining U.S. influence over world politics, coupled with increasing Japanese assertiveness and the strength of a post–1992 Europe powered by a united Germany at its core, will have important implications for Latin America. With its strongest patron losing power in world arenas, will Latin America also lose some visibility and clout, or will a more united and energized Western Hemisphere emerge as a result?

These questions will be at the core of Latin American concerns over the next decade. Any attempt at resolving them, of course, should begin with the United States—the undisputed leader among creditor governments involved in the region. Latin America has traditionally been viewed by all and sundry as a region of U.S. domination (for better or worse). It is in the backyard of the United States, just as Eastern Europe is next door to Western Europe and Asia is increasingly coming under Japan's sphere of influence. Interestingly, the 1990 summit of Western leaders in Houston, Texas, saw these roles confirmed: Germany insisted on providing aid to the Soviet Union, Japan did likewise for China, and the United States made a feeble plea for more aid to Central America.

THE U.S. GOVERNMENT ROLE

U.S. policy toward Latin America has evolved through three fairly distinct phases after some initial fumbling, from the Baker to the Brady Plan to the Enterprise for the Americas Initiative of President George Bush. The Baker Plan, defined in 1985 by then Treasury Secretary James Baker, called for additional bank lending to countries engaged in large-scale economic restructuring. Essentially just a restatement of well-established standard procedure, the Baker Plan provided little impetus for new development and resulted in an evermounting pile of foreign debt for Latin America. This led to the promulgation of the Brady Plan in 1989, named for Bush's Treasury Secretary Nicholas Brady, which shifted the focus to debt reduction for countries with approved economic reform programs. This plan, too, however, foundered on a lack of commercial bank support as debt agreements concluded under its aegis proved to be glacial in pace and meager in benefits for debtor nations.

With the Brady Plan, too, under sharp criticism for falling short of expectations despite the earnest efforts of many debtors to introduce economic reforms, the newest wrinkle is Bush's Enterprise for the Americas Initiative. This program amounts to an extension of the Brady Plan and is designed to quell Latin American criticism of the Brady Plan and reassure Latins that Bush's commitment to the region is not waning. The new initiative foresees the eventual creation of a free-trade zone in the Western Hemisphere, envisions substantial debt relief on official U.S. credits to Latin America, and sets aside funds for a new program to be administered by the Inter-American Development Bank to foster private investment. It represents an attempt to lift Latin America out of its decade-long economic stagnation, bolster recent moves toward democracy, and provide opportunities similar to those being offered Eastern Europe.[2]

The evolution from Baker to Enterprise reflects shifting U.S. policies and priorities toward Latin America. For one thing, as fears of communism recede other political goals are gaining in importance. The Bush government has come to believe that a new generation of leaders is emerging in Latin America (Salinas in Mexico, Fujimori in Peru, maybe Collor in Brazil, and even Menem in Argentina) who are genuinely committed to economic reforms and the creation of a free-market economy. With elections now over in much of the region, a radical leftist surge has not materialized; the debt issue has not become unduly politicized; and the need now is to bolster the newly elected governments. Thus, the U.S. goal is to reinforce the changes already made, regenerate growth by easing the debt burden, and help create a sense of hemispheric identity. This represents a sharp break from the Reagan years, during which concern was centered on the national security threat posed by insurgents backed by the Soviet Union and Cuba. U.S. interest in ideological contests in Central America is waning as the Cold War ends, giving way to new interest in integrating Latin American economies into the developed world. In the process, the government hopes to create a strong and united Western Hemisphere that can serve as an effective counterweight to the Asian and European monoliths.

Thus, U.S. interest in fighting the perceived communist threat in Latin America is being replaced by an awakening sense of its economic interest in a stronger region to the south. In 1980, the U.S. ran a trade surplus vis-à-vis Latin America; by 1990, this had turned into a $10 billion a year deficit. The government wants its companies to recapture these lost markets, especially as fears of a post–1992 Fortress Europe are building. Latin America still has a combined gross domestic product more than two-thirds that of Eastern Europe and the Soviet Union, and the region accounts for 5 percent of world trade. With the U.S. government breaking free of its Cold War blinkers, it is now proposing that U.S. economic and security interests in Latin America are best served by guaranteeing a prosperous region governed by sound macroeconomic policies.

This shift in U.S. government policy emphasis is both encouraging and promising. However, the government encounters a number of constraints when it comes to implementation. First of all, the huge U.S. budget deficit is a seriously binding constraint, especially when coupled with declining U.S. ability to pressure its Western allies to ante up on behalf of Latin America. With the budget deficit greatly exceeding its Gramm-Rudman-Hollings targets and a savings-and-loan crisis now expected to cost more than $2,000 for each taxpayer in the country, the United States is severely strapped. Discounting narcotics-related aid, U.S. assistance to Central and South America has been declining steadily due to budget problems and the position of traditionally favored states such as Israel, Egypt, Pakistan, and the Philippines (again, reflecting perceived U.S. strategic interests in those regions). Hope is fading that the so-called "peace dividend" to be achieved through lower defense spending will increase resources for foreign aid. More likely, it will mean less reductions for current recipients as the savings from defense cuts will primarily be used to help reduce the overall deficit in line with Gramm–Rudman demands.

These problems are illustrated by Bush's Enterprise for the Americas plan, which sets forth lofty goals while pledging very small financial commitments due to the budget constraint. Moreover, the program will need substantial backing from Congress as well as a strong commitment from Europe and Japan. Bush has been sending strong messages to the rest of the G7 leaders that he is seriously interested in Latin America. However, the message is clearly being drowned in the sea of concern for Eastern Europe. Latin American leaders continue to sharply criticize the United States for allowing Eastern Europe to drain Western aid programs and attention; however, U.S. ability to refocus world priorities is clearly limited.

Bush not only must deal with reluctant and disinterested Western allies on the issue of Latin debt policy, he must also cope with the various interests within his own government. Controversy frequently erupts between the Treasury Department and the Federal Reserve Board, Congress and the president over how much support to provide for the struggling debtors, and to what extent the government should be involved in what is perceived as a bailout of the banks. The Treasury and Fed have clashed repeatedly, for instance, with the latter concerned that Brady Plan emphasis on debt-principal reduction would result in insufficient new credit becoming available for developing countries.

A well-publicized and embarrassing row between the Fed and Treasury developed over U.S. involvement in the commercial bank deal concluded between Mexico and its bankers in early 1990. In order to close the deal, the Treasury was forced to sell bonds with a face value of $33 billion to Mexico at prices alleged to be well below market value in exchange for similar zero-coupon bonds. The arrangement reduced Mexico's initial payment and greased the way for a final agreement with bank lenders. Congressmen charged that the deal included a hidden subsidy to Mexico and its bankers, and were heartened by a General Accounting Office (GAO) finding that the deal involved "an effective subsidy of approximately $192 million."[3] Treasury officials countered with the argument that U.S. taxpayers should contribute to Mexico's economic renewal; fortunately, public outrage over the savings-and-loan bailout appears to be swamping this contretemps.

With the U.S. government at odds with itself as well as its Western allies, a final weakness remains: its ability to pressure commercial banks. Bush's Enterprise is laudable for finally addressing the issue of outstanding government credits to developing countries. However, this is of minimal importance to Latin America, where over 60 percent of foreign debt is owed to commercial banks. Brazil,

Chile, and Mexico owe nearly 80 percent of their debt to bankers, and Argentina is close to 85 percent and Venezuela hovers close to the 95 percent mark. Thus, government ability to manipulate commercial bankers is another crucial element its policy toward Latin debtors, and here again the U.S. record is decidedly mixed. Relations between leading international bankers and the U.S. Treasury have deteriorated markedly since the introduction of the Brady Plan, as bankers see themselves as the pawns of U.S. foreign policy—especially with regard to Mexico. With the Treasury viewing Mexico as a test case of its new policy and traditional U.S. interest in its southern neighbor intense, the government was heavily involved in negotiations between Mexico and its commercial bank creditors in 1989–1990. As noted before, the Treasury's sale of bonds to Mexico was ultimately necessary to clinch the deal. Moreover, government and banking officials conceded that the Treasury aggressively arm-twisted banks to ensure that they would ante up with new loans to Mexico, leaving a sour taste in many bankers' mouths. In October 1989, for instance, a "senior Treasury official" was widely quoted as saying that if the debt agreement between Mexico and the banks was not concluded, it would be renegotiated on worse terms for the banks.

Mexico, however, is a special case for the United States given the myriad trade and investment ties between the two countries as well as Mexico's critical geographic position on the southern flank of the United States. Successive U.S. governments attach great importance to Mexico; in August 1989, for example, Bush took four Cabinet-level aides to Mexico for a series of talks. Mexico has taken on even more importance recently as the testing ground for the Brady Plan to manage Latin American debt; hence, the heavy government involvement in its negotiations despite the official policy of noninterference. In fact, the Brady Plan negotiations have focused on countries of strategic importance to the United States, such as Mexico and the Philippines. The question is, though, how other big debtors such as Argentina and Brazil will fare without the same claim on U.S. government attention. As *The Financial Times* editorialized in January 1990, " . . . even the modest benefits gained by Mexico would not have been possible without strong U.S. intervention. Whether such support will be exercised on behalf of other debtors is doubtful."[4]

Additionally, it is shortsighted to behave as if the United States holds all the cards necessary to solve the Latin American debt problem. As U.S. efforts to secure the support of its Western allies indicate, broadbased attention and funding from Japan and Western Europe are also required. Bush's Enterprise plan, for example, provides for the United States to contribute $100 million to a fund aimed at assisting reforms toward the development of free markets. The goal is to seek matching contributions from Europe and Japan to create a total fund of $300 million.

WESTERN EUROPE'S ROLE

With regard to Western Europe, of course, the key issue is to what extent its preoccupation with Eastern Europe will crowd out Latin American interests over the next decade. In this context, it is illuminating to consider the decision of Mexico's President Salinas to pursue free trade with the United States following a lengthy visit to Europe. In his address to the World Economic Forum in early 1990 during this journey, Salinas pointed out that Mexico had already carried out many of the reforms still being urged in Eastern Europe. He pled: "May these splendid signs of change not cloud Europe's global vision, nor turn its attention away from our continent—particularly Mexico—and from other regions of the world."[5]

Throughout the Mexican leader's trip, he complained of European "fascination" with events in the Eastern bloc and of its "relative lack of attention to other parts of the world." However, he was ultimately convinced after meetings with German Chancellor Helmut Kohl and Prime Minister Margaret Thatcher of the United Kingdom that Mexico could not hope for significant flows of European aid or investment over the next few years. Considerably sobered by his wanderings, Salinas concluded that Mexico could not realistically hope to use Europe or Japan as a counterweight to the United States. His bottom line was, therefore, enthusiastic support for a free-trade zone with the United States and maybe even Canada.[6]

Any examination of government priorities within Western Europe could not fail to conclude that Salinas is not far off the mark. European politicians are indeed preoccupied, even obsessed, with the emergence of Eastern nations from communism. As *The New York Times* acknowledged in June 1990: "President Salinas is acting fast to reform his economy. But global forces keep moving faster."[7]

President Bush was singularly unable to divert the attention of his Western allies from East European issues during high-level meetings throughout 1990, and the trend appears to be accelerating rather than easing off. This is especially evident with regard to the West European leaders. West Germany is still the third largest investor in Mexico, but seems destined to lose this position as its funds are increasingly diverted to Eastern bloc nations. U.S. Treasury Secretary Brady has openly criticized the Germans for building up large trade surpluses but not being as generous in aiding debt reduction as the Japanese, but these protests are falling on deaf ears. As for France, while Mitterrand is under pressure to prove himself a friend of the poor, French moves toward debt reduction are primarily focused on the Francophone countries of Africa.

Some hope is held out, however, by the traditionally close relationship between Latin America and the Iberian countries of Spain and Portugal. These countries (and Italy to a more limited extent) have gradually strengthened their ties over the past decade. Spain and Mexico, for instance, have signed a $5.5 billion trade and investment deal to cover the first half of the 1990s, and companies are discussing joint ventures and other forms of business cooperation. Spanish banks outdid the Brady Plan in 1990, writing off some 50 percent of Mexico's debt as opposed to the 35 percent eventually achieved in the agreement with U.S. commercial banks. The year 1992 should be pivotal, marking the advent of full EC integration and the 500th anniversary of Columbus' arrival in the New World.

Many Latin Americans have come to look on Spain as a welcome and valuable counterweight to U.S. influence as well as a gateway to the EC. However, on the other hand, many also fear Spain is losing interest in its former colonies in its eagerness to become a full, modern member of Europe. Spanish entry into the EC in 1986, for instance, required it to relinquish its preferential trade agreements with Mexico and other Latin American countries, resulting in a significant decline in relations. On the other hand, however, Spain and Portugal are more threatened than stimulated by the rising tide of Eastern European economic power, unlike the stronger Western countries, and thus are more likely to maintain interests in Latin America. Thus, despite lingering anxieties related to Spain's colonial past, on the whole, political and economic ties with Latin America are strengthening.[8]

Western Europe on the whole, though, has made little more than token responses to Latin American concerns. In mid–1990, the EC proposed an ECU 2.9 billion package of aid to Latin America and Africa, an increase of 80 percent over previous levels of support. This was seen as a demonstration of the European determination not to allow events in the East to swallow a disproportionate share of its resources. The EC has also indicated its interest in shifting emphasis from traditional forms of development aid to increased economic cooperation with more dynamic developing regions, such as Latin America. Responding to U.S. pleas for more aid to the region, the EC vice president for external affairs reassured that the EC response would be "positive and constructive." Such bureaucratic doublespeak, however, does little to reassure nervous Latins that West European leaders will have much time or money for them in the next decade.

THE JAPANESE ROLE

As a result, Latin American eyes may turn further east with hope that Japan will pick up the slack left by U.S. budgetary constraints and European indifference. Japan has become a significant investor, trade partner, and aid giver for Latin America, with long-term interests in the region, especially among Pacific Coast countries. It is evident that the Japanese government is keen to take an active role in world development in general, and Latin American development in particular. By 1990, Japan had become the world's largest aid-giver. It has committed $50 billion in foreign assistance between 1988 and 1992, which is concentrated in Southeast Asia, but also includes an increasing component earmarked for Africa. Believing that the newly industrialized countries of Asia that have been receiving Japanese aid will soon reach a level of development at which they will reduce their dependence on foreign capital, the government is trying to refocus its priorities so that more aid in the future will go to truly developing countries.

As another step in the process of taking a more assertive role in world development, the Japanese government has been aggressively seeking to increase

its influence over international financial institutions that have long been dominated by the United States and Western Europe. Japan is moving to promote a
candidate to run the IMF when the term of its current director expires in 1992.
Japan has become the second largest shareholder in the World Bank, and has
also moved to second place within the Fund.

These efforts reflect a desire to improve Japan's world image as well as its
determination to pursue economic interests in the Third World. The Japanese
have been stung by charges that they are amassing hundreds of billions of dollars
in trade surpluses, as well as criticism that Japanese businesses pursue environ-
mentally unsound practices in their worldwide operations, specifically by financing logging concerns in South America that destroy rain forests. The
government aims to reverse the image of Japan as a hard-working and efficient
but essentially self-centered society by coming forward with massive amounts
of aid for the developing world.[9]

Accordingly, Japan has provided hard cash to assist in the debt-reduction
effort, winning praise from Treasury Secretary Brady at least, and the Ministry
of Finance has pledged full support for the Brady Plan. In mid–1989, Japan
vowed to make up to $10 billion available for debt reduction in Latin America
and elsewhere in the Third World. As part of the 1990 Mexican debt agreement,
Mexico will receive the largest portion of this money (some $2.05 billion in
new loans).

As with the United States, though, this reflects the special position of Mexico
and may not bode well for the rest of Latin America. There is no doubt that
Japanese–Mexican ties are strong and getting stronger. Mexico's relationship
with Japan has become one of its most important bilateral tie, including a wide
array of linkages between the private and public sectors. For Japan, Mexico is
attractive both as a market of 85 million people and as a gateway to the United
States and Latin America. It also does not hurt that Mexico has oil to sell; Japan
is Mexico's third largest buyer of crude oil. Since 1982, Japanese private direct
foreign investment in Mexico has doubled, becoming the country's second largest
trade partner and creditor. On the other side, Salinas sees Japan as the only
remaining counterweight to U.S. power and is himself something of a Japano-
phile; his children attend Japanese-language schools in Mexico City.

Thus, it is not surprising that the Japanese government, like the United States,
has become a willing partner in the effort to allay Mexico's external debt problems. As part of the 1990 debt deal, the Japanese Ministry of Finance agreed
to arrange a special issue of 30-year bonds to Mexico's government, which will
be used as collateral to secure new Mexican bonds. In addition to Japan's role
in restructuring Mexican debt, the Export–Import Bank of Japan has pledged to
make available loans to Mexico to help it buy new bonds and repay credits. In
mid–1990, following a successful visit by Salinas to Japan, the Japanese government agreed to extend development loans of $1.6 billion (mostly devoted to
pollution control), which more than doubles the total amount of credit made
available by Japan from its initial announcement. These moves signal Japan's

willingness to take a direct, active role in resolving the Latin debt crisis—at least insofar as Mexico is concerned.

But although the Japanese government may be convinced that it should be a player in Latin America, the private sector is less sanguine. Business leaders in Japan have politely, but firmly, expressed their reservations about increasing investment in Latin America, complaining of insufficient clarity and the potential for bureaucratic arbitrariness. Japanese commercial banks are choosing to extract themselves from Third World debt. Partly thanks to enlarged tax benefits offered by the Ministry of Finance, most commercial banks chose not to lend more funds to Mexico as part of the 1990 debt deal, opting instead to take advantage of the tax benefits with substantial write-offs of existing credits. And again, Mexico is clearly a special case for the Japanese government; there is every reason to believe that its interest in and generosity toward Latin countries with less obvious economic advantages will be correspondingly less impressive.

Nonetheless, it would be unfair to deny that governments of industrial countries have indeed made important concessions to the indebted nations in 1988–1990. Many governments have converted aid loans into grants. At the 1988 Toronto Summit, Western leaders agreed on a formula to allow debt relief for the poorest African countries; 1989 saw the adoption of the Brady Plan that encouraged the use of IMF and World Bank resources to encourage banks to write off loans to middle-income debtors. Governments have thus shifted focus from further raising debt toward debt reduction, but official strategy is still "full of anomalies and contradictions," according to a May 1990 *Financial Times* editorial.[10]

A key sticking point has traditionally been the issue of official debt to Third World nations. While persuading commercial banks to accept less than 100 cents on the dollar for their credits to middle-income debtors, governments have been reluctant to do the same for their own official export credits. Government-to-government debt is rescheduled under the auspices of the Paris Club, and so far creditor governments have resisted forgiving trade debt except to the poorest African countries. Thus, in the eight years since the infamous Mexican weekend, almost all efforts in both the private and public sector have concentrated on debt owed to commercial banks. At the same time, the problem of huge sums of debt owed by Third World countries to Western governments has mounted, as the freedom to forgive export credits is constrained by the consensus that prevents countries from gaining advantages over each other through aggressive export-credit subsidies.

By mid–1990, though, the political argument in favor of official debt for-giveness had become insurmountable and the problem was on its way to reso-lution. Bush built into his Enterprise for the Americas Initiative his intention to write off substantial amounts, in some cases more than 50 percent, of the out-standing principal of $7 billion in concessionary loans. The United States also plans to push for reduction of bilateral debt obligations on a case-by-case basis for countries following IMF reform programs. The United States alone can make a significant dent in the official debt burdens of Latin American countries, since the U.S. government accounts for 90 percent of official (i.e., noncommercial bank) debt of these countries.[11]

Even so, as noted before, Latin America is heavily weighted toward commercial debt. The largest countries owe at least 70–80 percent of their debt to commercial banks. Thus, while movement toward forgiveness of official debt is a welcome sign, it is only an incremental step toward reducing the debt burden of the most important Latin American countries.

The more critical issue of ongoing support from creditor governments remains open. One measure of such support is the regulatory framework created by creditor governments to deal with the debt crisis. In this context, Brady stressed when promulgating the Brady Plan that "creditor governments should consider how to reduce regulatory, accounting, or tax impediments to debt reduction where these exist." It is fair to say that U.S. monetary and regulatory authorities have been flexible in interpreting tax and supervisory provisions to aid in implementing the Brady Plan. European and Japanese authorities, however, have favored banks taking increased loan-loss provisions through tax deductibility, in turn strengthening the banks in these countries, but also providing no tax incentive to accept reductions in principal or debt-service levels. Tax regulations in Europe, Canada, and Japan, therefore, encourage provisioning against loan losses, but not debt reduction. The difference over regulatory issues highlights basic differences in priorities and concerns with regard to the entire debt issue.[12]

THE ROAD AHEAD: THE 1990s

The U.S. government's approach to Latin American debt over the next decade will probably vary from country to country, reflecting its strategic and economic interests in each nation as well as approval or disapproval of its economic and political policies. This framework will result in strong support for Mexico, while Argentina and Brazil will be far less fortunate. Nonetheless, rising U.S. interest in Latin America bodes well for the region as a whole, in reaction to U.S. fears of a Fortress Europe coupled with the growing Japanese hegemony over Asia. Severe budgetary constraints and divisions within the government, though, will dilute the effectiveness of U.S. policy in this area to a considerable extent.

Prospects for support from West European governments for Latin American debt-resolution efforts are correspondingly dim. Western European governments will be willing, even eager, to write off official debt and thus rid themselves of the nagging headache that these create. Except for Spain and Portugal, however, the Europeans will be much too preoccupied with themselves to devote much attention and resources to Latin America beyond token displays of interest.

This leaves Japan somewhere in between the strong U.S. commitment to Latin America and European indifference. Japan's desire for a world leadership role in the 1990s will conflict with a reluctance to get heavily involved in expensive bailouts of what may be perceived as Latin American basket cases. The wide gulf between Japanese and Latin American cultures will make the process of rapprochement more difficult. In the end, Japanese support for Latin America will probably vary from country to country in response to the potential wealth and investment prospects to be found. Again, Mexico will be the key beneficiary of Japanese interest, whereas the more problematic and frustrating countries such as Argentina and Brazil will win only sporadic support.

NOTES

1. This point is illustrated by the Harvard Business School case study by Philip A. Wellons, *Managing the Debt Crises of Developing Countries* (Cambridge, MA: Harvard University Press, 1981).

2. See Andrew Rosenthal, "President Announces Plan for more Latin Debt Relief," *The New York Times*, June 27, 1990; or "Enterprise of the Americas," *The Financial Times*, July 2, 1990.

3. "GAO Says Treasury Underpriced Bonds That It Sold to Mexico," *The Wall Street Journal*, August 14, 1990.

4. "Mexico's U.S. Connection," *The Financial Times*, January 6, 1991, p. 4.

5. Quoted Alan Riding, "Mexico's President Urges Latin Investments by West," *The New York Times*, February 1, 1990.

6. See, for example, the article by Larry Rohter, "Free-Trade Talks with U.S. Set Off Debate in Mexico," *The New York Times*, March 28, 1990.

7. Larry Rohter, "Stop the World, Mexico Is Getting On," *The New York Times*, June 3, 1990.

8. See Nicholas Bray, "Spain's Rediscovery of Latin America Spurs Hopes of Co-operation, Partnership," *The Wall Street Journal*, August 2, 1990.

9. This point is illustrated frequently in the Financial Times Survey of Japan, July 9, 1990.

10. "Solutions for the Debt Problem," *The Financial Times*, May 16, 1990.

11. Stephen Fidler, "Forgive But Not Forget," *The Financial Times*, July 6, 1990.

12. Stephen Griffith-Jones and Roy Culpeper, "Regulatory Issues and the Brady Plan," *The Financial Times*, November 22, 1989.

3   Actors in the Latin American Debt Crisis II: International Financial Institutions

Allen M. Rodriguez*

INTRODUCTION

Since the early 1980s, all Latin American countries have wrestled with severe adverse external circumstances that have been exemplified by sharp contractions in lending by foreign banks, high real-world interest rates, and a deterioration in prices of raw materials. Latin American nations were extremely vulnerable to the external shocks as they had accumulated a heavy stock of external debt, and had based its repayment on overoptimistic assumptions on world interest rates, access to international credit, and their export performance. Also, until the early 1980s, large net commercial bank inflows supported consumption and investment far in excess of domestic production. Accordingly, each Latin American nation, to one extent or another, was forced to adopt policies to stabilize and structurally adjust their economies.

Pivotal roles in the process of stabilization and adjustment in Latin America have been played by the International Monetary Fund (IMF) and the World Bank (the International Bank for Reconstruction and Development or (IBRD), the two principal international financial institutions (IFIs). The Inter-American Development Bank (IDB) also channeled significant multilateral project credits to the region during the 1980s. Both the IMF and World Bank have helped Latin American countries to design and implement macroeconomic programs

*The author is a senior international economist with the U.S. Treasury Department and was the financial attache (1986–1989) to the U.S. Mission, OECD, Paris. The views expressed herein are solely those of the author, unless otherwise indicated.

to cope with weakened economic and financial situations. The IFIs have sup-ported stabilization and adjustment programs with loans conditioned on economic performance. With the shift of the international debt strategy in early 1989, the IMF and IBRD assumed the additional role of providing support for voluntary, market-based debt and debt-service reduction transactions. This chapter surveys the recent activities of the IMF, the World Bank, and the IDB in the application of the international debt strategy to Latin America and assesses the prospective contributions of these institutions.

IMF'S ROLE VERSUS THE WORLD BANK

The IMF has traditionally focused its overall efforts on providing short-term assistance to member countries confronting temporary or, in rare cases, persistent balance of payments difficulties. In essence, the adjustment to the balance of payments requires countries to adopt measures to bring their current account in line with long-term capital flows and transfers. The IMF's loans are extended on the principle of "con-additionality," that is, to qualify for loan disbursements, the country must meet strict quantitative macroeconomic targets. Latin American countries seeking the IMF's assistance have frequently faced a large public-sector deficit, excessive monetary creation, an overvalued exchange rate, minimal levels of foreign-exchange reserves, and binding constraints on borrowing from commercial banks and other foreign creditors.

The IMF works with officials in the country (typically, in the Finance and Planning Ministries and the Central Bank) to design and implement a stabilization program to alleviate the imbalance in the country's external accounts. The pro-gram seeks to address root causes of the problem; in many cases, excess aggregate demand is determined to be the main culprit. Once the member country agrees with the Fund on a package of adjustment measures, the IMF extends short loans (i.e., repayment in 3 to 5 years) or medium-term loans (i.e, repayment in 4½ to 10 years) in support of the agreed economic package to bolster the country's international credit worthiness.

Until the advent of the debt crisis in mid–1982, the World Bank, in turn, concentrated primarily on project-specific lending to Latin American countries to promote development and alleviate poverty over the medium term. Project lending still accounted for 77 percent of total World Bank lending to Latin America and the Caribbean in 1990.[1] Since 1982, however, the World Bank has worked closely with the IMF to help Latin American countries design policies for macroeconomic stabilization and structural reform. The World Bank has supported these policies with economywide lending programs and, more recently, policy-based sectoral loans. The IDB will provide, for the first time, policy-based sector lending with cofinancing from the IBRD during 1990–1992.

A critical by-product of the new collaboration between the IMF, the World Bank, and the IDB on the formulation of stabilization and structural reform programs for Latin American and Caribbean countries has been the reinforcement of conditionality arising from the combination of credit facilities. The cross-linkage between institutions and lending programs has strengthened the economic reform programs of the recipient governments.

IFI'S ROLE IN LENDING TO LATIN AMERICA

In recent years, there was a strong upward swing in lending by the IFIs to Latin America, in contrast to the fall in commercial bank exposure. In 1982, total outstanding loans to Latin American countries from the World Bank/IDA amounted to $8.5 billion; by 1985, these loans had risen to $12.2 billion, and they skyrocketed further to $25.4 billion by mid–1989. Between 1985–1989, disbursements by the World Bank (net of principal repayments) to Latin American countries amounted to $8.6 billion.[2]

The increase in the World Bank's exposure in Latin American and Caribbean nations, however, has also led to higher interest and other charges incurred by these countries to the World Bank. Starting in 1988, there were substantial net transfers (i.e., interest and principal repayments exceeding disbursements) by Latin American and Caribbean countries to the World Bank: in 1988, there was a net transfer of $362 million; net repayments escalated to $1.2 billion in 1989.[3]

In 1990, however, this pattern was reversed with a net transfer of $1 billion from the World Bank to Latin America, despite net repayments by Brazil and Argentina totaling $920 million. Argentina's and Brazil's large net repayments to the IBRD were largely offset by $2.4 billion in net IBRD transfers to Mexico in 1990.[4]

Large net transfers from Latin American and Caribbean countries to the IMF have also occurred in recent years. In the year running through April 1989, net reimbursements from Latin American and the Caribbean countries to the IMF amounted to about $810 million and $25 million, respectively. A principal factor accounting for the imbalance was numerous countries' inability to meet targets in their IMF adjustment programs and to qualify for disbursements.[5] As of July 1990, for example, total outstanding commitments by the IMF for Latin America and the Caribbean amounted to $6.1 billion, of which only $3.8 billion had been drawn.[6] In the year through April 1990, however, there were net disbursements from the IMF of $796 million to Latin America and the Caribbean, primarily on the basis of $1.9 billion in new IMF credits to Mexico.[7]

CURRENT WORLD BANK PROGRAMS

As noted before, the debt crisis plaguing Latin America has significantly altered the World Bank's traditional focus on promoting development and alleviating poverty. IBRD loan programs aimed at structural adjustment of the overall economies, or of specific sectors, have emerged to help Latin American countries implement substantial reform measures. In 1989, for the first year ever, the World Bank's so-called "nonproject" lending accounted for the largest single share of IBRD lending to Latin America and the Caribbean. A variety of other IBRD financing arrangements have recently been created that have assisted Latin American countries, most notably cofinancing facilities, programs to enhance debt and debt-service reduction, lending to promote private-sector development, and insurance of inward capital flows to foster foreign direct investment.

ADJUSTMENT LENDING

At present, the World Bank provides support for structural adjustment of Latin American economies through Structural Adjustment Loans (SALs) and Sectoral Adjustment Loans (SECALs). Both loans are designed so that all tranches, or portions, can be quickly disbursed. SALs involve comprehensive, economywide programs aimed at reforming the country's trade regime, pricing of public goods, and public expenditures and revenues. In their emphasis on overall macroeconomic reform, SALs parallel the macroeconomic "conditionality" of an IMF standby facility. SECALs, in contrast, are aimed at making a specific sector of the economy (i.e., agriculture, finance, trade, industry and energy) more efficient and competitive.[8]

Both sectoral adjustment loans and structural adjustment loans require that recipient countries implement specific adjustment measures as a precondition for disbursement of tranches of the loan. These might include raising energy prices, cutting agricultural subsidies, and lifting nontariff barriers. Unlike project lending, SALs and SECALs can be utilized to finance nonproject imports and fill a country's balance of payment financing gap in the same manner as Fund credit.

SECALs have recently replaced SALs in many Latin American nations as their authorities have found it easier to enact sector-specific reform measures.[9] In effect, the IMF has been left with the sole responsibility among the IFIs for ensuring that overall macroeconomic policies in Latin America countries are appropriate to achieve sustainable economic growth.

In exchange for implementation of economy- or sectorwide economic policy reforms, the World Bank has provided quick disbursing SALs and SECALs to a number of Latin American nations. To date, twelve Latin American countries have received such loans with Brazil and Jamaica the most active, each receiving three SALs or SECALs.[10]

The World Bank candidly acknowledges that performance under SALs and SECALs has been mixed and is difficult to measure.[11] In exchange for SALs, Chile and Mexico significantly altered their trade regimes by exchange-rate depreciation, and cutting export restrictions. Chile's authorities, however, had already implemented a variety of adjustment measures when the Bank's first adjustment loan was extended in 1985. Steps taken included reforms of the financial system and the social security system. Both Chile and Mexico have reached relatively advanced stages in their economic reform programs. Little additional structural reforms are possible. Consequently, World Bank assistance is likely to revert to solely project lending for both countries.

In Colombia, the World Bank provided critical support for an adjustment program with a SECAL in 1985 and another in 1986. Impressive results were achieved in exchange-rate adjustment, export liberalization, and fiscal policy. The World Bank's SECALs, in combination with Fund monitoring, were a unique and successful arrangement for Colombia, and were a critical factor in the resumption of commercial bank lending to Colombia. Under the Fund–Bank framework, Colombia successfully negotiated a $1 billion commercial bank financing package in 1985–86. An additional $1 billion commercial bank facility was successfully negotiated in 1987–88 after disbursement of the second SE-CAL.[12]

With Mexico, a variety of SECALs have been extended in support of ambitious trade-liberalization measures. The first SECAL was provided in 1983, and was followed by two trade policy loans in 1986 and 1987 amounting to $500 million each. SECALs for agricultural reform and similar operations for steel and fertilizer were extended. Jamaica, in turn, received annual SALs or SECALs from 1981–84 coupled with net drawings from the Fund.[13]

ENHANCEMENT OF DEBT
AND DEBT-SERVICE REDUCTION

In late May 1989, the World Bank and IMF adopted operational procedures for debt and debt-service reduction. As the World Bank notes, its support and the Fund's for private bank debt and debt-service reduction is at an early stage, and only experience will show how such assistance affects Latin American and other debtor nations.[14] In a nutshell, the World Bank and the Fund agreed to provide credits to guarantee the portion of Latin American debt to banks remaining after debt and debt-service reduction. In this way, both organizations would play a key role in the reduction of the private debts held by Latin American countries.

The first mechanism, referred to as "set-asides," allows the Latin American country to apply up to 25 percent of the World Bank's adjustment lending per year (or 30 percent of IMF lending) for cash buybacks by the country of its debt to creditor banks or to back discount or par bonds to reduce principal or interest payments on bank debt. Second, the countries can apply 40 percent of their IMF quota and about 30 percent of IBRD program and project lending projected over three years to buy par bonds to support reduction-of-interest payments. In 1989, the Fund approved arrangements for Costa Rica, Mexico, and Venezuela that include provisions for debt and debt-service reduction.[15]

The Mexican financing package, signed in February 1990, constituted an early example of the complementary roles that the World Bank and IMF will play in promoting debt and debt-service reduction programs in Latin America. The financing package offered Mexico's creditor banks with two options for exchanging their existing medium-term debt to commercial banks for debt and debt-service reduction programs. The first option—debt reduction bonds—replaced existing medium-term commercial bank debt at a discount of 35 percent.

The second option consisted of debt-service reduction instruments carrying annual interest rates fixed at 6.25 percent.

Facilitating Mexico's debt and debt-service reduction schemes were a three-year, $3.5-billion Extended Fund Facility with the IMF and a $6-billion World Bank lending program, including an estimated $4.5 billion in policy-based sector loans in support of Mexico's economic adjustment. These credit facilities, in conjunction with another $2 billion and $1.3 billion from the Governments of Japan and Mexico, respectively, provided a total of $7 billion in set-asides, or enhancements, for reduction of Mexico's debt and debt service to creditor banks. Specifically, about $1.1 billion and $750 million from the IMF and World Bank credit facilities, respectively, were "set-aside" for purchase of 30-year zero-coupon bonds to back debt-reduction bonds. In turn, the IBRD and IMF provided an additional $950 million and $600 million, respectively, for support of interest reduction.

In May 1989, the IMF also approved a standby arrangement with a 25 percent set-aside for debt reduction and the possibility of additional Fund resources of up to 40 percent of Costa Rica's quota for debt reduction. The IMF approved a similar arrangement under Venezuela's Extended Fund Facility arrangement in June 1989.[16] At the same time, a World Bank Structural Adjustment Loan (SAL) and a trade reform loan totaling $402 million and $353 million, respectively, were approved for Venezuela. Up to 25 percent of $100 million of the quick-disbursing funds from the SAL could be applied to debt reduction; the World Bank's trade reform loan contained similar conditions.[17]

In his speech on June 27, 1990, President Bush proposed that the IDB join the IMF and World Bank in providing set-asides for commercial bank debt reduction by Latin American and the Caribbean countries. These funds would also be linked to programs of macroeconomic reforms.[18]

Cofinancing

Cofinancing is an arrangement by which private creditor banks and export-credit agencies have participated in development projects with the World Bank. A number of cofinancing credits have been extended by the IBRD to Latin American countries in recent years. In several instances, the IBRD has helped arrange a syndicated loan with private banks and has taken on a share of the loan. In 1989, the World Bank provided $2.7 billion in cofinancing credits to Latin American and Caribbean countries to supplement a total of $985 million from private commercial banks and $1.2 billion from official export agencies.[19]

Boosting the Private Sector

The International Financial Corporation (IFC), an affiliate of the World Bank, aims to promote economic development of developing member countries by supporting the growth of their private sectors and strengthening their capital markets. The IFC traditionally has granted private companies direct loans, and, more recently, has assisted companies in the restructuring of their debts. The IFC has also helped promote privatizations.

In South America, the IFC has recently focused on assisting export-oriented private companies engaged in resource-based manufacturing. For example, the IFC has provided two private Chilean firms with loans totaling $80 million to process wood pulp for export.[20] The IFC, in turn, has provided Argentine and Bolivian private firms with loans to conduct oil recovery and metallic mining, respectively.[21]

In 1989, the IFC also assisted the Visa Group, one of Mexico's largest industrial conglomerates, which was overburdened by debt, to develop a menu of debt-reduction options that trimmed $1.3 billion off Visa's corporate debt and cut $1.1 billion off Mexico's outstanding debt.[22]

In addition, the IFC has taken steps recently to deepen the domestic capital markets in several Latin American countries by taking positions in country-specific international mutual funds. In 1988, the IFC took a $63.2 million equity position in The Brazil Fund, Inc., a new closed-end investment fund launched on the New York Stock exchange that invests in publicly traded Brazilian securities. The IFC also provided a $7.6-million equity investment to capitalize the Chilean Investment Company, a debt-equity conversion fund financed by the Chilean Central Bank that invests mainly in publicly traded Chilean securities. In 1989, the IFC also helped establish a $50-million debt-equity conversion fund for Argentina.[23]

In 1989, the IFC subsequently invested $12.5 million in The New World Investment Fund, a privately placed fund headquartered in the United States that allows U.S. institutions to invest in Latin American stock markets.[24]

Foreign Direct Investment

In addition to loans from the World Bank and the IFC promoting foreign investment, the Multilateral Investment Guarantee Agency (MIGA), an affiliate of the World Bank, is also working to promote foreign direct investment in Latin America and other developing countries. Established in 1988, MIGA promotes equity and other direct-investment flows to developing countries by providing guarantees (typically, for a period of 15 years) to foreign investors against losses caused by "noncommercial" risks.

The types of risk that MIGA protects foreign investors against include: currency transfer; expropriation; war, revolution, and civil disturbance; and breach of contract. At present, only three Latin American countries (Chile, Ecuador, and Guyana) and three Caribbean nations (Barbados, Grenada, and Jamaica) are members of MIGA. Additional membership by Latin American countries in MIGA could trigger substantial inflows of foreign direct investment into Latin American and Caribbean nations. However, the deep-seated resistance in many Latin American countries to the concept of international arbitration of investment disputes, as embodied in the Calvo Doctrine, will have to be overcome in order for more countries to join the MIGA.

CURRENT IMF PROGRAMS

The IMF has played a key role in promoting balance of payments stabilization among Latin American countries since the advent of the debt crisis in 1982. A key target in nearly all recent Fund programs for Latin American countries has been a sharp contraction in the size of the nonfinancial public-sector deficit. The Fund's prominent role in helping Latin American countries to formulate economic policies to overcome the external crises—and the occasional increase in unemployment—has at times triggered harsh nationalistic outbursts and riots. In 1984, for example, more than 900 riots in Rio de Janeiro, Sao Paulo and other Brazilian cities were aimed at the IMF, the alleged culprit responsible for rises in unemployment and price increases.[25]

In the last several years, the IMF has become even more active and flexible in lending to Latin American countries. For example, the Fund adopted in 1989 the policy, in certain instances, of disbursing to Latin American and other developing countries in advance of the debtor countries' reaching agreement with creditor banks on a financing program and, in some cases, in the presence of external arrears. Breaking the link between an IMF program and the elimination of arrears in certain cases might help facilitate participation of banks in debt and debt-service reduction programs.[26] In May 1989, the IMF agreed to make its support for debt and debt-reduction operations conditioned on compliance with standby or extended facility arrangements.

Latin American countries' maximum annual access to Fund resources (i.e., their "IMF quota") is determined by the size of their economy and contribution to the IMF. Among Latin countries, Brazil currently has the largest quota (SDR 1.5 billion) followed by Venezuela (SDR 1.4 billion), Mexico (SDR 1.2 billion), and Argentina (SDR 1.1 billion).

As of July 31, 1990, eleven Latin America and Caribbean nations had formal arrangements with the Fund. Of this number, eight countries (Argentina, Chile, Ecuador, Guyana, Haiti, Honduras, Jamaica, and Trinidad and Tobago) had standby arrangements, two extended fund facilities (Mexico and Venezuela), and one enhanced a structural adjustment facility (Bolivia).[27] A standby arrangement for El Salvador was subsequently approved in August 1990.[28]

Standby Arrangements

The principal source of IMF financial assistance provided to Latin American and Caribbean nations has been by means of so-called standby arrangements, normally ranging in duration from 12 to 18 months. Disbursement of each portion, or tranche, of the standby facility is "conditional" on economic performance, that is, the drawdown of credits depends upon the recipient country meeting in advance a variety of quantitative macroeconomic performance targets. Full repayment, notwithstanding the country's balance of payments situation, is required within 3¼ to 5 years.

Principal emphasis is placed on the variables that reflect the economy's fiscal and monetary performance and, to a lesser extent, exchange rate adjustment. Standby programs typically focus on the size of the public sector deficit as a share of the gross domestic product, the overall borrowing requirement of the public sector, and the net domestic assets of the Central Bank.

In an innovative approach, standby arrangements were approved for Chile and Venezuela in 1989 that allowed a conditional drawdown of credits limited to the first credit tranche. This treatment mirrored both countries' relatively strong economic and financial situations and their improving prospects for a return to voluntary lending from private banks.

Extended Fund Facility Arrangements

Created in 1974, the Extended Fund Facility (EFF) Arrangement furnishes credits for up to three years (in exceptional cases, for four years with greater access) and in larger amounts than under standby arrangements. Repayments are also stretched out to 4½ to 10 years. Countries eligible for the EFF are those experiencing balance of payments difficulties stemming from structural imbalances in production, trade, and prices, or whose development is hampered by weak balance of payments conditions. A three-year, SDR 3.3-billion EFF was approved for Mexico in May 1989 and a three-year, SDR 3.7-billion EFF for Venezuela was approved in June 1989. The IMF's program for Venezuela supported President Perez's austerity program that eliminated price controls, multiple exchange rates, and state subsidies.[29]

Enhanced Structural Adjustment Facility (ESAF)

The ESAF, created in late 1987, is a concessional Fund lending facility to help very low-income countries facing protracted external payments problems to adjust their policies and grow over the medium term. The ESAF's loans are repayable over ten years at a current interest rate of one-half of one percent. Sixty-two of the world's poorest countries are eligible to apply for ESAF loans.[30]

Bolivia is the only Latin American country that has been a recipient of an ESAF facility. In December 1989, the IMF approved the second year of Bolivia's three-year ESAF. The 1990 phase of the ESAF, equivalent to $58.2 million, aims at an economic growth rate of 4 percent and further cuts in inflation from 14 percent in the year that ended in September 1989 to 9 percent in 1990. A central element of the program is the reduction of the public-sector deficit to 3.3 percent of the GDP, from an estimated 5 percent of GDP in 1989 and 6.7 percent of the GDP in 1988.[31]

Bolivia's medium-term ESAF encompasses a variety of structural reforms, including liberalization of the trade regime, strengthening the tax and customs administration, restructuring an accelerated privatization of public enterprises, and legislative changes to encourage private-sector investment in the mining and hydrocarbons sectors.

Enhanced Surveillance

Under the program known as enhanced surveillance, the Fund, at the request of a member country, closely monitors the country's economic performance and quantitative financial program. Members that request this IMF program have a good track record of adjustment and do not require the IMF's financial assistance. A principal goal of enhanced surveillance is to assist the country in concluding a multiyear rescheduling with its country's creditor banks and to facilitate the member's return to voluntary borrowing. In 1988, Colombia had a program of enhanced surveillance with the IMF that aided it in its efforts to return to voluntary lending from its commercial banks.

Compensatory and Contingency Financing Facilities (CCFF)

Established in August 1988, the CCFF replaced the Compensatory Financing Facilities, which permitted member countries to borrow from the Fund when they experienced balance of payments problems beyond their control because of temporary shortfalls in their export earnings and an excessive rise in the cost of specific cereal imports. The CCFF kept most features of the CFF, but added a "contingency" mechanism that allowed countries with standby or EFF programs that might be disrupted by external factors (sharp changes in export or import prices, unexpected rises in international interest rates) to qualify for additional credits from the Fund.

Jamaica received a CCFF in 1989 in the wake of the devastation associated with a tropical hurricane. Mexico and Venezuela were earlier recipients of similar IMF assistance to cover unexpected shortfalls in oil revenues. In January 1989, the Fund approved its first CCFF for Trinidad and Tobago. It covered potential export-price shortfalls for a combination of exports (petroleum, steel, methanol) and to ensure against changes in international interest rates.[32]

CURRENT PROGRAMS OF THE INTER-AMERICAN DEVELOPMENT BANK

Composed of forty-four members (twenty-five Latin American and Caribbean countries, the United States, Canada, Japan, Israel, and fifteen European countries), the IDB provides three basic lending windows to its Latin American and Caribbean members: ordinary capital (OC), the Fund for Special Operations (FSO), and the Inter-American Investment Corporation (IIC). Policy-based sector lending will now be provided for the first time under the IDB's OC window.

FSO loans are provided at concessional interest rates to the region's poorest countries.

The IIC, in turn, was established as an IDB affiliate in 1986 to support private-sector activities in Latin America and the Caribbean. After considerable delay, the organizational phases of the IIC were completed in late 1989. In the last several months of 1989, the IIC conducted its first five operations for a total of $14.9 million in Argentina, Brazil, the Dominican Republic, Mexico, and Uruguay.[33]

The total lending volume by the IDB stood at a record $2.6 billion in 1989 compared to $1.7 billion in 1988. Among borrowing nations in the IDB, Brazil and Mexico have been the largest recipients of IDB credits—$6.7 billion and $5.1 billion, respectively—since the IDB began its operations in 1961.[34]

During the 1990–1993 replenishment period, the IDB will begin a program of policy-based sector lending. Fast-disbursing, policy-based lending is new to the IDB. The IDB will not undertake broad-based structural adjustment lending, but will focus instead on loans aimed at improving the economic efficiency of specific sectors such as agriculture. For the first two years of the 1990–1993 replenishment period, all IDB sector loans will be cofinanced with the World Bank.

At present, there exists no program of IDB policy-based lending to enhance debt and debt-service reduction, although President Bush, in his June 27, 1990 address on the Enterprise for the Americas Initiative, called for the creation of such an arrangement.

LATIN AMERICAN ARREARS TO THE IFIs

With regard to the World Bank, five Latin American countries out of a total of nine World Bank member countries had payment arrears in February 1990 in excess of six months. The countries were Guyana, Honduras, Nicaragua, Peru, and Panama. Because interest and/or principal on these loans was substantially past due, the IBRD's disbursements were halted and substantial loan-loss provisions were established. Four of the five Latin American countries, excluding Nicaragua, also had overdue obligations to the IMF, whereas all of the group, except Guyana, had arrears to the IDB.

Several of the five Latin American countries were formally declared ineligible to use the general resources of the Fund in light of their arrears.[35] As of November 30, 1989, Honduras was declared ineligible due to some $25 million in overdue obligations to the IMF. Guyana had been declared ineligible since May 15, 1985, because of arrears totaling about $140 million.

The normalization of Guyana's relations with the Fund was the first case of a full settlement of arrears to the Fund and the removal of ineligibility. Under the so-called "intensified collaborative approach," Guyana's creditors and donors established a group that provided special financial assistance to Guyana in support of a comprehensive economic adjustment program. An arrears-clearing program supported by bilateral bridging assistance followed shortly after for Honduras. After clearing their arrears to the IMF in June 1990, Guyana and Honduras both regained their eligibility to use IMF resources.[36] The IMF and IBRD subsequently both began discussions with authorities from both countries. Standby arrangements for both countries were approved in July–August 1990.

After a more than three-year suspension in debt servicing to the IFIs and private banks, the government of Peru took preliminary steps in December 1989 to normalize its relations with the IMF. It paid $42.3 million to cover its fourth-quarter 1989 obligations to the IMF. Peru's remaining arrears to the Fund, however, are estimated at about $800 to $900 million. Given the magnitude of Peru's arrears, the IMF's "rights" approach might be the most appropriate mechanism for dealing with Peru's arrears to the IMF. Endorsed by the industrialized members of the IMF in May 1990, the "rights" approach would involve an IMF-monitored program of about three years. If the country successfully completes its program, it would then qualify for disbursement of the first tranche under a new arrangement.[37]

IFI RELATIONS WITH LATIN AMERICA: FUTURE PROSPECTS

In the 1990s, there is likely to be a further absolute increase in IMF, World Bank, and IDB lending to Latin American and Caribbean countries. The potential magnitude of flows from the IFIs to the region in the 1990s, however, is difficult to calibrate. Clearly, the major share of new lending by the IBRD and IDB will continue to be in the form of project lending. This will particularly be the case for countries like Mexico and Chile, where most macroeconomic and structural reforms have been completed and opportunities for new policy based lending are increasingly limited.

For those Latin American countries implementing macroeconomic and structural reform programs, the IFIs will also extend additional credits conditioned on economic performance. A substantial amount of these IFI credits could be applied to help reduce debt and debt service to creditor banks.

In the 1990s, the prospect also looms of increasing differentiation (and possible de facto separation) in the lending strategy pursued by the IFIs in the region. For countries such as Chile and Mexico, which are completing ambitious structural and sectoral reforms, the IBRD is likely to revert to traditional project lending geared to basic economic development. IMF credits in these countries may be limited (with perhaps access only to the first credit tranche) or entirely phased out depending on the country's external financing situation. The declining levels of IMF assistance coupled with a fall in nonproject lending by the IBRD would imply a sharply reduced role for the IFIs in debt and debt-service reduction.

In contrast, other Latin American countries in the relatively early process of reform are more likely to be recipients of substantial policy-based lending from the IBRD and IDB coupled with project lending. The focus will be more on structural reform rather than traditional project lending aimed at economic development. IMF assistance will probably remain an important component, particularly in light of limited access by these countries to private international capital.

Finally, the issue of transfers to the IFIs is a key consideration for Latin American countries in the 1990s. Many remain net capital importers due to chronic balance of payments deficits associated with inadequate domestic savings. A modest net transfer from the IFIs to Latin America in the 1990s might yield very positive economic results, particularly since many of the countries appear to be firmly committed to ambitious free-market reform programs.

NOTES

1. The World Bank, *Annual Report, 1990* (Washington, D.C.: The World Bank, 1990).

2. The World Bank, *Annual Report, 1989* (Washington, D.C.: The World Bank, 1989).

3. Ibid.

4. The World Bank, *Annual Report, 1990*.

5. International Monetary Fund, *Annual Report, 1989* (Washington, D.C.: IMF, 1989).

6. *IMF Survey*, Vol. 19, No. 17, September 10, 1990.

7. IMF, *Annual Report, 1990* (Washington, D.C.: IMF, 1990).

8. The World Bank, *Adjustment Lending, An Evaluation of Ten Years of Experience* (Washington, D.C.: The World Bank, Country Economics Department, December 1988).

9. Ibid.

10. Ibid.

11. Ibid.

12. Ibid.

13. Ibid.

14. World Bank, *World Debt Tables, Volume 2, 1989–90* (Washington, D.C.: The World Bank, December 1989).

15. *IMF Survey*, Vol. 19, No. 3, February 5, 1990.

16. IMF, *Annual Report, 1989*.

17. The World Bank, *Annual Report*, 1989.

18. June 27, 1990: Enterprise for the Americas Initiative speech by President Bush.

19. The World Bank, *Annual Report*, 1989.

20. International Finance Corporation, *Annual Report*, 1986–1989.

21. Ibid.

22. Ibid.

23. Ibid.

24. Ibid.

25. See Richard Feinberg, *Debt and Democracy in Latin America* (Washington, D.C.: Overseas Development Council, 1989).

26. *IMF Survey*, Vol. 19, No. 5, March 5, 1990.

27. *IMF Survey*, Vol. 19, No. 16, August 13, 1990.

28. *IMF Survey*, Vol. 19, No. 17, September 10, 1990.

29. Ibid.

30. *IMF Survey*, Vol. 18, No. 23, December 11, 1989.

31. Ibid.

32. *IMF Survey*, Vol. 19, No. 9, May 7. 1990.

33. Inter-American Investment Corporation, *Annual Report, 1989*.

34. Inter-American Development Bank, *Annual Report, 1989* (Washington, D.C.: Inter-American Development Bank, 1989).

35. *IMF Survey*, Vol. 18, No. 23, December 11, 1989.

36. *IMF Survey*, Vol. 19, No. 13, July 2, 1990, and *IMF Survey*, Vol. 19, No. 14, July 16, 1990.

37. *IMF Survey*, August 1990, Supplement to the Fund.

4 Actors in the Latin American Debt Crisis III: The Domestic Actors

Jane Hughes

INTRODUCTION

The identification of important actors in debtor countries and a discussion of their position and power with regard to the country's willingness and ability to repay its external debt form a key step in our analysis of prospects for Latin American debtors in the next decade. With the return of democracy to Latin America has come a sharp increase in the number and strength of various domestic actors involved in the debt crisis. In part, this reflects the increasing politicization of the debt crisis. The 1980s saw the triumph of the ballot box over military rule throughout the region; whereas at the dawn of the decade, over one-half of Latin America's population was under military rule, this figure has dropped to under 10 percent by 1990. Argentina, Bolivia, Brazil, El Salvador, Guatemala, Uruguay, Chile, and Paraguay all made the transition to full democracies during the decade, leaving Cuba as the only surviving personalized, military-backed regime. Most strikingly, during 1989, elections were cleanly fought and debated in Brazil and Chile. The remarkable sight of a dictator ousted by the ballot box in Chile illustrated the totality of the democratization movement in Latin America.

These historic events took place, however, against an increasingly gloomy economic background. With very few exceptions, the new democratic governments in Latin America failed to implement effective economic programs. It is true that leaders were largely preoccupied by the democratic transition and the building of new democratic institutions. Nonetheless, the performance of the new governments gave some credence to the claim that totalitarian regimes make better debtors (witness the decline in Eastern Europe's creditworthiness following the outbreak of democracy).

Although this chapter will not attempt to adjudicate that claim, it is certainly clear that democracy in Latin America has increased the number and power of various players involved in the debt crisis within the domestic arena of debtor countries. Nowadays, a list of actors in any given country who affect the debt crisis would include politicians of all stripes, labor leaders, domestic business (large, medium, and small), even novelists, television personalities, pop singers, drug traffickers, and urban guerrillas. Rule by democracy means that all of these actors affect the debtor country's response to its debt problems, particularly the country's ability to implement economic adjustments.

A key issue in analyzing future creditworthiness, of course, is the extent to which a country can implement economic reforms to help it service external debt and satisfy the demands of international creditors. This, in turn, leads us to focus on each domestic actor's attitude toward economic reforms such as opening up the economy to foreign trade, competition, and investment; paring down the state sector through privatization, reduced subsidies, and layoffs; and trimming inflation through strict austerity policies. This chapter will accordingly analyze each actor's position on economic reform and debt service according to the PRINCE system of guidelines established by Drs. William Coplin and Michael O'Leary.[1] The PRINCE system assesses each actor as follows:

1. Orientation: the current general position of an actor toward economic liberalization and debt service, classified as positive, negative, or neutral (of course, there are many shades in between).

2. Certainty of orientation: the firmness or assurance of an actor's position. For group actors, such as labor unions or political parties, certainty is a function of the extent to which there is a consensus among the actor's membership in supporting or opposing the action.

3. Power: the degree to which an actor can exert influence, directly or indirectly, in support of or in opposition to an action. The basis of an actor's power and the ways in which power may be exercised are varied. Power may be based on such factors as group size, wealth, resources, institutional authority, prestige, and political skill.

4. Salience: the importance that an actor attaches to supporting or opposing the action, relative to all other relevant actions and issues with which the actor is concerned.

DEBTOR GOVERNMENTS

With this model in mind, we can now turn to the first and most obvious actor in the Latin American debt conundrum: debtor governments. It should be noted, however, that a government is far from monolithic on any issue, especially one as controversial and multifaceted as foreign debt. Each government contains a set of distinct actors, each with his own individual orientation, power, and salience on issues affecting the country's willingness and ability to repay its debt. Consider, for example, the United States government, where concerned actors would include the president, the Congress, the Federal Reserve, the State Department, the Commerce Department, and the bank regulators. These parties have different stakes in the matter, ranging from stability of domestic banks to promotion of U.S. exports to protection of U.S. jobs. The multiplicity of actors within the government in many Latin American countries is further complicated by the dynamics of the relationship between the head of state and Congress, the federal bureaucracy, and the ruling party. Although all of these actors are ostensibly part of the government, in fact, they may be deeply divided in many countries.

The relationship between the president and Congress is particularly thorny. The legislature and/or "ruling party" are often at odds with the president on the issue of foreign debt. Many Latin American democracies have adopted a presidential system that invests enormous powers in one individual for a fixed period in office, leading to fears of "creeping authoritarianism" as a result. Furthermore, this creates a system that depends heavily on the personality and quality of the president, while reducing the role of Parliament (or Congress) as a debating forum and increasing institutional tensions between the legislature and head of the government.

The nearly universal Latin American practice of using jobs in the government bureaucracy as a source of patronage has also created armies of underemployed, easily corrupted public servants who can routinely block implementation of measures even after they have been passed by president and Parliament. Thus, a high level of tension among president, party, legislature, and bureaucracy within the government will characterize virtually every country to be discussed in this chapter.

THE MEXICAN GOVERNMENT

Discussion of specific debtor governments may as well commence with the country where economic reform has gone furthest, Mexico. The accomplishments of President Salinas de Gortari are substantial and impressive in the areas of trade liberalization, opening to foreign investment, and paring down the state sector through an ambitious program of privatizations. These accomplishments were crowned with a historic debt accord in early 1990 under the guidelines of the Brady Plan, which aims to cut Mexico's debt burden by around 20 percent. All of these gains combine to give Mexico a reasonable hope of achieving moderate, low-inflation growth in the 1990s.

Nonetheless, these gains also mask deep and bitter divisions within the government over the very foundation of Salinas' reforms, which have created fears about the direction of future policy. Salinas is currently running the country with a group of like-minded technocrats and the "dinosaurs" or old-style party bosses. The president believes that his Institutional Revolutionary Party (PRI) must break its identity with the government if it is to become a modern, democratic party.

Traditional party leaders, however, are loath to surrender their privileged position and tight relationship with government and labor. This tension is reflected in the contradictory actions taken by Salinas, who has allowed some opposition triumphs in local elections but suppressed others through brazen electoral fraud. With the entire Congress up for reelection in 1991, the PRI could lose its majority if free elections are permitted. This could permanently split the PRI, bringing Salinas into alignment with the rightwing National Action Party (PAN), whose policies are closer to his than those of the PRI old guard in any case.

These political tensions could become an increasing problem in Salinas' efforts to maintain a steady economic course. The 1990 debt accord, despite the praise heaped on it by both the United States and Mexican governments, is hardly a panacea for Mexico's ills. Nonetheless, Salinas has staked much credibility on his vow to reduce debt-service payments through "negotiation not confrontation," withstanding pressures from inside his own party and Congress for just such a confrontation. Ultimately, his fortunes rest on his ability to manage the economy and negotiate a deal that will permit the regeneration of growth following a decade of austerity. Visiting a desperately poor Mexico City suburb in January 1990 to celebrate the introduction of electricity and water service, Salinas proclaimed: "This is why we renegotiated the foreign debt!" The question remains, however, how long he can maintain this stance in the face of an accord that provides precious little real debt relief.

In this light, it is worth noting that Salinas has already launched an ambitious $1.3 billion public works program that he calls "Solidarity." He plans to substantially hike spending on health, education, and food subsidies. The likely cost of these plans, however, exceeds the amount that he will realize from lower debt service and privatization of state enterprises. This dilemma reflects the constant danger of pressure from within the PRI and Congress, which may push Salinas away from reform and austerity measures needed to maintain payments on Mexico's foreign debt.

THE ARGENTINE GOVERNMENT

A glance at the Argentine government, though, makes the friction within the Mexican government look like a lighthearted family squabble. President Menem took office as the head of the Peronist Justicialist Party, whose basic tenets include economic nationalism and general state control of the economy. Upon taking office, however, Menem was forced into a situation where prices were doubling every week, foreign reserves were drained to virtually zero, no payments had been made on foreign debt in over a year, and hyperinflation had already sparked food riots. His immediate actions went sharply against the Peronist heritage and put him in a state of guerrilla warfare against his own party and legislature.

Menem took steps to reduce the state's deficit through tax reform, control of government spending, and, the most controversial of all, the selloff of state companies—all in hopes that Argentina would be able to renew its frayed relationship with the IMF and renegotiate its foreign debt. In deciding to turn toward private enterprise, however, Menem now stands accused of betraying Peronism. His legislative efforts have been diluted by Peronist politicians, leaving them full of loopholes and much less effective than he had hoped. The party is essentially dividing between those who support Menem and those backing his longtime opponent Antonio Cafiero, who demands a reversal of the privatization drive. This has managed to stall vital legislation in Congress, where the Peronists only hold a majority in the Senate.

As of this writing, Menem appears ready to confront his own Peronist Party to pursue economic efficiency and will attempt to rein in the party's renegade politicians. He has fewer advantages in his battle against party traditionalists than does Salinas, however, thanks to a weaker economy, weaker power base, and stronger opponents. The likely outcome appears to be a breakdown of party lines and a new set of political alliances that will separate Menem from his Peronist foes. The question of whether Menem is truly an economic pragmatist or merely an opportunist, however, is still open. The danger is that he may still cave in eventually to the entrenched forces that will always oppose opening the economy to foreign competition. He moved swiftly at first because he had little choice given the economic disaster confronting his country, but this does not mean that he is equipped or eager for a drawn-out confrontation with this own party.

THE BRAZILIAN GOVERNMENT

The Brazilian situation is somewhat different, because here the president has virtually no party of his own to contend with although he does face a feisty legislature. President Collor has introduced a set of dramatic policies aimed at slashing the state's role in the economy along with inflation (which totaled over 4,500 percent in the year before he took office). His explosive economic reforms include deregulation, privatization, and import liberalization along with a hotly debated freeze on domestic deposits constituting about 70 percent of the money in circulation. With respect to foreign debt, despite much rhetoric about the "tough stance" he will take in debt talks, all indications are that Brazil will return to the negotiating table and hammer out a deal based on economic reforms under the Brady Plan principles.

Collor faces a number of weighty obstacles to his dream of integrating Brazil into the developed world economy. He lacks a party base, as his tiny party commands barely 5 percent of the seats in Congress and looks unlikely to increase its standing dramatically in the next congressional elections. Nonetheless, he must persuade Congress to go along with his radical economic measures by gathering a coalition behind him in the legislature. He must also confront the "rights" of job-secure civil servants, subsidized farmers, wealthy industrialists, and other powerful vested interests in his quest to modernize and streamline the economy.

These efforts are further complicated by the new constitution adopted in 1988, which sharply limits the executive's power. At the same time, this highly idiosyncratic document closely protects the privileges of various special interests, for example, guaranteeing a minimum wage, limiting real interest rates, and protecting inefficient state industries. Thanks to the constitution, Collor is (at least on paper) the weakest head of state ever; he requires congressional approval for each detail of economic policy. In particular, Congress moved in late 1989 to impose further restraints on the president's ability to negotiate foreign debt deals. Among other things, the Congress voted a restriction on interest payments to a ceiling of 6 percent per annum; it rejects New York as a venue for the discussion of debt issues; and it refuses to accept a penalty clause for nonpayment in any new accord.

Although these Alice-in-Wonderland conditions could probably be bypassed by the president, they could also be used as an excuse for an intransigent negotiating stance. Most important, they underline how determined the Congress is to wrest power on this issue from the president, especially the right to sanction or veto future debt accords. In general, legislators have proved to be a deeply conservative force, with the right wing protecting vested interests and the left wing defending workers rights. They constitute a massive obstacle to Collor's ambitious blueprint for change and reform.

During the early days of the Collor administration, however, open battle was averted as a nervous Congress approved most of the new president's economic plan. Collor has, so far, managed to unite the center right parties behind him in Congress. Despite the failure of his hopes for a "cross-party alliance," he can still gather a clear majority in Congress with a coalition absorbing all of the parties to the right and a sizeable hunk of the ill-defined Democratic Movement Party (PMDB).

The future relationship looks to be much trickier, however. Collor will find it difficult to hold together such disparate groups once the atmosphere of acute economic crisis fades. Moreover, Congress was nervous facing elections set for late 1990. When the Collor honeymoon cools and a new Congress emerges after elections, lawmakers will probably be decidedly more feisty. Most important, Collor's biggest asset in his early days was the economic disaster confronting Brazil. Hyperinflation had produced a near consensus that without swift action to reduce the yawning state deficit, implement reforms, and privatize state enterprises, Armageddon loomed.

Many future measures, however, will require amendments to the constitution, which in turn requires a three-fifths majority in Congress. Collor may discover that nothing short of an economic apocalypse will deliver this level of support. Also, Brazil is inching toward a parliamentary system of government in the 1990s, which raises the intriguing possibility of a Prime Minister Lula cohabiting with a President Collor. What worked well in France between the Socialist

Presidency of François Mitterrand and right-wing Prime Minister Jacques Chirac in the 1980s could produce paralysis in Brazil. In the meantime, Collor must rely on a shaky center–right coalition and the strength of his personality. But much of what contributed to his electoral success—youth, outsider status, and independence from traditional parties—could become an obstacle to his plans once in office. In the worst-case scenario, an institutional crisis could erupt between the executive and legislative branches of government, leaving Brazil virtually ungovernable.

THE CHILEAN GOVERNMENT

The Chilean governmental experience over the past decade presents a disquieting model for Latin America, as dictatorship has unquestionably wrought wonders for the economy. Under Pinochet, Chile boasted Latin America's best economic record with respect to growth, inflation, and debt management. The new democratic government, however, faces pent-up demands for social improvement that will be difficult to fulfill without backpedaling on the progress that Chile made in the 1980s. This reflects the sorry fact that prosperity in the 1980s through liberalization and privatization benefited only a few, while income distribution and living standards for the poorer half of the population deteriorated. The new president, Patricio Aylwin, in fact, campaigned on a promise to increase spending on social projects and wages. Moreover, Aylwin faces the challenge of holding together Socialists and Christian Democrats in the new government. His coalition includes a strong contingent of socialists who have opposed Pinochet's open-market policies, increasing pressures on the president and producing fears that he will be a slave to his leftist allies.

However, there are also strong forces at work in Chile for a continuation of economic policy under the democratic government. In fact, the elections revealed a near consensus: even Aylwin insisted throughout the campaign that he would leave most of his predecessor's economic policies intact. He benefits from the examples before him of other countries where new democratic governments rushed to improve wages and social services (witness Argentina and Peru), but state deficits and hyperinflation eventually provoked a sharp recession. Aylwin is also very conscious that economic traumas frequently end in military takeovers, and is determined to avoid this trap. Moreover, the Socialists hope to prove that they can govern responsibly, without creating economic disasters. Finally, before leaving office, Pinochet ensured that the central bank would be autonomous and impervious to the political process in its control over money supply, use of foreign-exchange reserves and policies on exchange rate and foreign debt.

Accordingly, all indicators suggest that the government will try to steer a course of improving social expenditures without swelling the fiscal deficit. Rather, it will use higher corporate income taxes and a value-added tax to finance social spending. The government is committed to maintaining the macroeconomic framework of the Pinochet years, while monetary policy is in the hands of the

autonomous and technocratic central bank. Thus, the proliferation of new domestic actors in Chile is not expected to upset the debt-management process.
The only victim may be Chile's successful debt-swap program, which was criticized during the Pinochet years for subsidizing foreign investors via large discounts. The program will not halt completely, but may be further limited, for
instance, to activities that increase exports or help Chile develop new markets
and technology.

OTHER DEBTOR GOVERNMENTS

Other Latin American governments similarly have tended to adopt (eventually!)
orthodox economic policies once in power, often putting the government into a
difficult position vis-à-vis its own party and legislature. Venezuela presents a
good example of a country where the president bowed to austerity once in office.
Before his election, Carlos Andrés Pérez was viewed by bankers as a populist
on the debt issue, reflecting his campaign rhetoric and record during his previous
administration. He was an avid bank basher during the campaign, and his 1974–
1979 administration was marked by poor economic management and free spending.

Once in office, however, Pérez implemented strict austerity and reform programs to open up the economy, privatize some of the state businesses, and cut
subsidies. Despite his criticism of foreign banks in speeches on the stump, Pérez
substantially eased his position by clearing up interest arrears and abandoning
his demands for a 50 percent debt-reduction package. This contributed to agreement in March 1990 on a debt deal that should reduce the debt burden under
the Brady Plan. Pérez, too, faces sharp opposition in his Congress over economic
policy, but appears to believe that given existing constraints, he has very little
choice but to embrace economic orthodoxy.

Even Peru, one of the international financial community's most notorious
pariahs, is starting to back down after four years of implacable opposition to
financial orthodoxy. Since taking office in 1985, President Alan García refused
to allocate more than 10 percent of export earnings to debt service. This produced
massive arrears in excess of $6 billion, and earned Peru a spot on the IMF's list
of countries ineligible for further lending. By early 1990, however, even Peru
had agreed to make a token payment to the Fund and to accept a shadow economic
program aimed at reducing inflation. Subsequently, the new president, Alberto
Fujimori implemented a new economic program in mid–1990 that inches toward
reform and liberalization.

OPPOSITION PARTIES

The opposite viewpoint is presented by oppositions throughout Latin America;
overwhelmingly, the opposition is more militant on debt policy than the ruling
party government in virtually every country. Obviously, foreign debt is an issue

with broad popular appeal: it is easy to blame foreign bankers and especially the old bogeyman of U.S. exploitation for a country's economic ills. Thus, it is not surprising that opposition groups throughout the region have seized on this issue and found it a formidable weapon against a government forced into unpopular austerity policies.

In Mexico, the debt crisis has proved a tremendous boon to the leftist opposition, which has made historic gains in the 1980s. The populist left accuses Salinas of selling out to foreign interests, reflecting Mexico's traditional, nationalistic distrust of foreign capital as well as real economic distress. The poor are undoubtedly reeling from a decade of austerity and stagnation, while economic policy for most of the period served to aggravate the vast disparities between rich and poor. Leftists found further ammunition in the debt accord negotiated in 1989–1990, which gives less relief than hoped. The growing Democratic Revolutionary Party (PRD) of presidential hopeful Cuauhtémoc Cárdenas asserts that Mexico will soon be back at the negotiating table in an even weaker position than before, and has renewed his call for a complete debt moratorium.

These positions have found great favor with the public. Cárdenas won (by official count!) 31 percent of the popular vote to Salinas' 50 percent in December 1989. Since then, PRI hegemony has continued to crumble with opposition wins or near wins in a number of local elections despite sometimes massive fraud by the PRI. This creates tremendous pressure on Salinas, who must demonstrate an ability to generate economic growth through attractive debt agreements before the 1994 elections.

Similar dynamics emerged in the Brazilian presidential campaign of 1989. Much of the election rhetoric told voters that resolution of the debt problem would relieve most of Brazil's economic woes. Only one candidate (who landed solidly at the bottom of the polls) advocated meeting debt payments out of exports, whereas the others advocated a range of policies from rescheduling to moratorium. Luis Ignacio da Silva ("Lula"), leader of the Workers Party and an almost successful presidential contender, proclaimed, "Our debt, by the hunger it provokes in our people, kills more people than wars."

Collor now faces a formidable opposition in Congress. The national executive of the Workers Party has decided to mount a "shadow" government along British lines to closely monitor the new administration. This group hopes to be joined by other left-twing parties and intends to offer "intransigent" opposition to the president. With regard to debt, the Workers Party advocates that Brazil halt all payments and use the money for agrarian reform.

Even "good" debtors such as Colombia and Venezuela have the same problems. In Colombia, the government's policy of prompt repayment has long been politicially unpopular as wage earners continue to lose ground. The opposition party urges the government to reschedule its foreign debt, arguing that if no fresh credit is available anyway, rescheduling would at least reduce the financial pressure and allow some increase in public investment. In Venezuela, official debt policy is increasingly unpopular. Unemployment has doubled to about 20 percent in mid–1990, while the economy contracted by 8 percent in 1989 due to tough economic policies implemented to mollify creditors. These problems produced riots protesting price hikes and food shortages in 1989, which caused 300 deaths, and during 1989, Venezuela also saw its first national strike in thirty years. The economic distress has also produced major gains for the opposition, which charges that Venezuela has seen no rewards for its struggle to maintain its debt payments. The ruling party lost eight of twenty state governorships to the opposition in December 1989.

Thus, we see that opposition parties have made great strides by criticizing the debt policy of more conservative-minded governments and urging more defiance of creditors. The question of whether this ultimately wins votes, however, is still open. Although Cárdenas and Lula did well, they did not win the elections. Bolivia, in fact, presents some evidence that austerity may actually win votes. The government there implemented an economic program of tough spending cuts, price liberalization, and deregulation that created severe hardships but also created a sense of optimism. In Chile, too, the winning candidate did not challenge the essence of Pinochet's free-market economic policies.

In this context, Argentina perhaps presents the most interesting if puzzling model. Here the "opposition" is coming from within the president's own party. There is a growing belief among disparate political forces that the country cannot support its public sector without foreign or domestic credit indefinitely. Despite the implacable hostility of Peronist traditionalists, privatization gets a 70 percent approval rating in public opinion polls. This may produce a pragmatic political accord between Menem and his Radical Party opponent in the 1989 presidential elections, with an anti-Menem coalition, including some members of the Radical Party, trade union leaders, and Peronist dissidents. This would create a similar pattern to those observed in Brazil, Mexico, Colombia, and Venezuela—where a pragmatic president is battling his populist opposition even though in the Argentine case the president is nominally Peronist.

LABOR GROUPS

Labor's position on external debt and economic policy is much less murky, presenting a tight front of anger at the government's subservience to foreign creditors. Labor generally allies with the opposition, even in Argentina, Venezuela, and Mexico, where the president presumably represents labor groupings. Most notably, in Mexico, labor increasingly appears to be set on a collision course with Salinas. Austerity has been the hardest on wage earners, who have seen the purchasing power of their salaries cut by 50 percent since 1980. This has contributed to their impatience with Salinas' willingness to seek a negotiated debt solution, rather than taking unilateral action like the debt moratorium urged by the leftist opposition. Labor leaders have forcefully criticized the 1990 debt accord, calling it inadequate and unjust while asserting that Salinas should have held out for at least 50 percent in debt reduction. Labor is also implacably opposed to debt/equity swaps and to the sale of state companies. For people in general and public employees of labor unions in particular, privatization means that life will become more expensive (for instance, through higher power, phone, and transportation rates). Adding insult to injury, privatization will also increase the role of foreign capital and influence in Mexico if foreigners take a large stake in the newly privatized companies. Thus it is not surprising that the labor movement constitutes Salinas' biggest challenge.

At the same time, labor is nominally part of the government party, the PRI. The labor movement itself, however, is deeply—probably irrevocably—split. Thus, the vital question becomes how far the state and PRI can continue to control the labor movement through the power of privileged union leaders. Veteran labor chief Fidel Valásquez (head of the 3 million strong labor federation CTM and a powerful member of the PRI executive committee) has reluctantly gone along with Salinas' economic program, including his tough wage and price controls. However, Valásquez faces increasing pressure at the grass roots level for high pay after years of austerity.

This, plus Salinas' own actions to weaken union bosses, has led to a deterioration in the party's formerly iron control over the workers movement. During his first year in office, Salinas engineered the removal of two long-time union leaders, including the head of the oil workers union, who is now in jail on murder, arms and corruption charges. These actions opened a Pandora's box of protest, emboldening long-smoldering dissidents in tightly controlled unions. By attacking the oil workers boss, Salinas inadvertently encouraged a real movement for union independence. As a result, strikes surged in early 1990 under the leadership of union dissidents. Further, a new trade union federation was formed by 121 union groups with the support of Cárdenas' left-wing opposition and Jesuit priests. The result will undoubtedly be more disarray in the labor sector, but the power of dissidents will rise inexorably in the labor sector and an eventual break with the PRI appears likely. The consequences of this shift for Salinas are immeasurable. He will no longer be able to count on even nominal labor support for his economic policies, meaning that a major ingredient in his successes to date has now been dissolved.

In Argentina, Menem, too, is heading for a confrontation with the unions, which have formed the bedrock of the Peronist movement. Many trade unions that played a leading role in Menem's victory now oppose his free-market policies. This is a gloomy signal, as economic stabilization policies in Argentina have failed for 45 years due to massive wage hikes. Moreover, the strongly nationalistic views of workers and their entrenched opposition to privatization collide head on with Menem's policy of conciliation with international bankers and the sell-off of state assets. His administration is now poised for a showdown with workers, as job actions are spreading to protest his determination to sell off/restructure state companies, promote exports, and hold down wages. The result, once again, is that just when Menem needs national unity, the trade union movement is dividing. The larger labor organization CGT (General Confederation of Labor) is splitting into two factions, with one group free to oppose privatization and press the government for higher wages. The strength of this anti-Menem faction is yet unclear, but it will form a dangerous and perhaps insurmountable obstacle to his plans for change.

Venezuela provides yet another example of a country where labor is aggressively confronting the government over its economic policies although the Federation of Venezuelan Workers (CTV) is controlled by a member of the president's party. Even so, the CTV asserts that the government's "foreign-inspired" economic program is creating inflation and unemployment; and in 1989, it sponsored the country's first nationwide general strike since the 1950s.

In Brazil, Collor is facing powerful unions linked to Lula, which are both radicalized and energized by Lula's strong showing in the elections. Moreover, these unions are directly threatened by Collor's plans, since their strongest position is within the state-controlled companies that are now slated for sale to new and possibly hostile private owners. Labor leaders are actively mobilizing resistance among civil servants due to be laid off, and will mount a strong opposition to Collor's economic platform.

BUSINESS

We have seen that in each country, labor is emerging as a big, probably the biggest, force confronting the government on its economic plans, even where labor is ostensibly linked to the government. Business, however, generally takes a more ambiguous stance on the debt issue and its position is often much more difficult to assess. On the one hand, business supports austerity, reform, and a conciliatory debt policy aimed at improving access to foreign capital, trade finance, and a stable economy. On the other hand, business is often threatened by measures taken by the government to further these goals. Big business possesses the resources enabling it to profit from economic chaos, including high inflation and low tax-collection efforts. Brazil, for example, boasts both soaring inflation and a booming private sector.

Big business is often dominated by the old postwar generation that profits comfortably by negotiating with the government and shows little interest in improving its competitiveness. The middle and upper classes are protected, and even benefit, from hyperinflation. With money invested in the United States, the wealthy grow wealthier and there is little inclination to repatriate the dollars invested in art, business, and real estate held abroad. Thus, it is not surprising that business leaders are often upset by plans to improve tax collection and hike value-added taxes. Moreover, the business community is fiercely opposed to price controls, and to competition to foreign companies as domestic economies are opened up to more trade and investment.

In Mexico, for instance, business leaders were delighted with Salinas when he won the election; now they are seriously divided over how much to cooperate with his economic program. The government has taken several actions that alienated the private sector, including the arrest of a multimillionaire businessman on charges of stock fraud, the imposition of a 2 percent asset tax on all corporations, the reduction of protective tariffs, and the implementation of wage and price controls. Moreover, business leaders politely argue that the debt accord under the Brady Plan does not provide what Mexico needs. They hope to avoid unilateral action to break the price freeze, but have warned Salinas that he cannot count on business sector cooperation indefinitely.

In Argentina, too, the alliance between Menem and big business groups had foundered by early 1990 under the weight of disputes over whether to free exchange rates and lower tariffs, as well as how to collect taxes. And in Brazil, business formed a solid core of support for Collor in the election, but now feels betrayed by his economic plans, including the arrests of shopkeepers for "economic crimes" (i.e., selling goods at prices above those set by the government). A pattern emerges: business nominally supports the new technocratic leader, but then is angered by specific reform policies and can become another obstacle to change. In fact, a major section of big business is usually at the center of a support coalition that forms around technocratic initiatives. Even while they quietly seek to evade austerity for themselves, big business often adopts a position of open support toward a stabilization program. On the other side, however, is a range of smaller business groups allied with military nationalists, unions and opposition parties against austerity.[2]

THE MILITARY

The military is generally an actor of declining importance in most Latin American countries, remaining well in the background for the most part, with the possible exceptions of Argentina and Chile. Also, the military's orientation on the external debt issue is difficult to assess. In general, the military has realized in country after country that it lacks the legitimacy to govern and has accordingly withdrawn from a direct government role. However, it has yet to establish for itself a clear alternate role, and by its continued presence emphasizes the very weakness of Latin American democracies. In fact, the military has become a powerful, and sometimes the most powerful, interest group in each country, forcing politicians to constantly look over their shoulders at the generals. In Argentina, for example, the recent army rebellions have been aimed not so much at overthrowing the government as achieving certain demands through force. The armed forces are angry over prosecutions, budget cuts on military spending, and economic chaos, much like any other interest group in the country. Indeed, there are hints of a growing alliance between the military and dissident Peronists aimed at ousting Menem.

Chile faces similar smoldering questions about the military's role in future governments. Pinochet is allowed by the constitution to function as a parallel government. The military is primarily concerned, however, with any efforts to prosecute for past abuses and is not fundamentally hostile to Aylwin. It is

certainly not inclined to interfere with economic policy unless substantial deterioration occurs.

The Brazilian military, too, is still an important political institution, reinforced
by the new constitution in its role as guarantor of law and order. The military
continues to see economic policy making as its prerogative and accepts austerity
policies only with great reluctance. As in other countries, the military's nationalistic views on policy are in some conflict with the government. In general,
Latin American militaries are thus still a key actor in the country. They are less
inclined to cooperate on austerity and debt negotiation than the government given
their nationalist leanings, but are also disinclined to take power once more. This
has transformed the military into a strong interest group rather than a potential
destabilizing force, although economic disaster could tip the scales toward military intervention once again.

DOMESTIC ACTORS ON DEBT ISSUES

Despite widespread delight at the return of democracy to Latin America, we
are forced to the conclusion that democratic governments have functioned
poorly with respect to economic policy in general, and debt policy in particular. Governments have become a strong force for change, but they are faced
with equally strong obstacles to change throughout the society, resulting in
economic mismanagement for much of the past decade. In the Spanish colonial tradition, special concessions and monopolies have been granted to particular enterprises, whereas others have received economic privileges in
partnership with the government. This tradition dies hard, and has constituted
a massive obstacle to change. First, private-sector leadership is often opposed
to free trade and is threatened by changes in its cozy relationship with the
state, which is a major buyer of goods and services. Second, trade unions
also defend established patterns of economic behavior and are usually cham-
pioned by opposition parties. Finally, the military presents a nationalistic
viewpoint that also opposes moves aimed at opening the economy to foreign
trade, competition, and investment.

The outlook is not unrelievedly gloomy, however. Against these conservative
forces are ranged a group of actors dedicated to liberalization and modernization.
A younger generation of managers and entrepreneurs has emerged, which is
providing some strong national leaders for the government. This explains the
pattern of a government at odds with the legislature and unions, which we have
observed throughout the region. Presidents tend to adopt similar policies regardless of their political stripes before they took office, confronting the opposition within their own party and legislature when necessary. Witness, for
example, the changes in the formerly promoratorium Menem and prodebt relief
Perez once they took office.

This dichotomy between forces for change, and obstacles to change, reflects
the difficulties of the new Latin American democracies while also explaining in

part why the results of democracy have been so disappointing thus far. Political leadership has been largely mediocre and self-interested, and governments have failed to establish adequate democratic institutions. The lack of a strong party base, for example, and the difficult constitution giving broad powers to a legislature controlled by powerful vested interests in Brazil have proved strong barriers to change indeed. The result: countries that have coped best are either relatively small (e.g., Bolivia and Uruguay) or run by authoritarian governments with strong institutions (e.g., Chile and Mexico). The depressing conclusion may be that Latin American democracies are not good for economic management. In discussing the downfall of communism in Eastern Europe, the *New York Times* noted in early 1990: "The move away from communism and toward market economies in Eastern Europe may be good news for the Europeans, but some Western bankers are getting nervous. . . . [This] is based not on opposition to greater freedom in the East, but on the expectation that new governments will do more to feed their people, and thus devote fewer resources to paying back debt."[3] Similarly, the evidence of the 1980s does suggest that dictators made better debtors in Latin America.

But as the 1990s dawn, there is also some evidence that governments in power tend to adopt very pragmatic policies eventually, regardless of who backed them originally. Thus, simultaneously with the return of democracy, there is a rising tide of economic reform in the region. This shift is certainly due to pragmatism and necessity rather than a basic shift in ideology. But even while it is a reminder of the very narrow range of options open to Latin governments given the debt crisis and fluctuating commodity prices, it is a welcome move nevertheless.

In fact, the current trend is without doubt in the direction of capitalist orthodoxy—a belief that open markets, free of government intervention, should determine economic performance. It has been dubbed "Thatcherismo" in Mexico, where a huge privatization program is underway. In Brazil, the new president favors privatization, an increase in foreign investment, and massive cuts in the state sector. It is nothing less than an intellectual revolution for Latin America to see proponents of both the right and left endorsing free markets as they discard state control of the economy and approach an entente with foreign creditors. There is a growing consensus that populist economics brought countries to the brink of ruin (such as Peru), and that debt relief begins at home with the need to greatly improve the investment climate. The urgency of this task is magnified by the fierce international competition for investment dollars as well as world attention from the newly emerging economies of Eastern Europe.[4]

Moreover, there is even some evidence of a growing ability to reconcile these goals with an understanding of the huge social costs of austerity. The plight of Latin America's poor has visibly deteriorated over the past decade as they have borne the brunt of economic adjustment programs, and social problems intensified in the 1980s. Thus, a mix of liberal economic attitudes toward trade, investment, and the budget deficit, plus a "left-wing" commitment to legitimize economic reform by ensuring that all sectors, especially the rich, bear the costs is emerging. The new Brazilian economic plan, for example, places its burden primarily on the wealthy, whereas Salinas in Mexico and Aylwin in Chile are committed to increased social spending without fiscal irresponsibility.

Not surprisingly, the new emphasis on encouraging private enterprise is being accompanied by a softening in Latin American rhetoric and militancy toward the debt issue. For one thing, foreign debt has lost credibility in some countries as the root of all evil (such as in Argentina and Peru), since these countries have not serviced their debt for years. Other countries such as Mexico can tentatively look beyond the debt crisis, hoping through the Brady Plan to obtain international support for a meaningful reduction in their debt burden. And the best off (Colombia, Chile) can even hope for new loans and normal relationships with creditors in the 1990s.

Thus, the commitment of Latin American countries to open markets, a sell-off of state enterprises, and policies aimed at attracting new capital and investment goes hand in hand with efforts to calm the debt crisis. But it is still unclear which and how strongly actors within a country are committed to these new, forward-looking policies, and this uncertainty creates some justifiable skepticism with regard to the longevity of these commitments. The 1990s will see a pitched battle between technocratic governments on one hand, and labor, opposition parties, and nationalistic military leaders on the other. The greatest danger is that the fanfare about debt-reduction negotiations under the Brady Plan will raise expectations that will not be fulfilled. This is a real concern, as even Mexico— a very special case given its strategic importance to the United States as well as its responsible debt-management policy—apparently received stingy treatment in its debt accord. Thus, the fear is that the international response to economic reforms in Latin America could be the weak link, eventually pushing the pendulum back to rule by populist, nationalist leaders.

Also, Latin American democracies still function poorly; political parties are drifting and fragmentation is a fact of life. Argentina, for example, may observe a political accord between the "opposition" Radicals and that section of the Peronist party still backing Menem. The rise of a new type of candidate with nonparty and clean government appeal is apparent, with outsider, even eccentric, candidates suddenly springing from oblivion into the limelight. Once in office, however, these candidates are handicapped by the need to deal with legislative bodies, as their outsider status becomes an obstacle rather than an advantage.[5] A fortuitous combination of strong, committed leaders and sufficient international support to keep a lid on tensions is therefore required for the 1990s. In Mexico, Salinas probably passes the first test and U.S. pressure will ensure that the second condition is met. Chile is likely to be another enduring success story. The jury is still out, however, on whether conditions in Argentina or Brazil will favor domestic actors who support reform, or those who will fight for their old privileges and perks.

NOTES

1. William Coplin and Michael O'Leary, *User Guide to Political Risk Services* (Syracuse, New York: Political Risk Services, a division of IBC USA, 1989), see Chapter 6, "The PRINCE Model."

2. See Robert Kaufman, "Democratic and Authoritarian Responses to the Debt Issue: Argentina, Brazil, Mexico," *International Organization*, Vol. 39, No. 3 (Summer 1985), pp. 323–349.

3. Floyd Norris, "Eastern Bloc Shift Worries Western Bankers," *The New York Times*, January 4, 1990, p. D1.

4. Annetta Miller, "Perestroika Goes South," *Newsweek*, November 6, 1989.

5. "Latin America's Next Decade," *The Financial Times*, December 29, 1989.

5   Actors in the Latin American Debt Crisis IV: The Commercial Banks

Paul Luke

INTRODUCTION

Without any doubt, Latin America was "bad news" for the international banking system during the 1980s. The Mexican moratorium of 1982 and its aftermath dragged commercial banks in nearly all major developed countries to the brink of collapse. It suited commercial banks, debtor nations, and industrial country governments alike to treat the crisis as one of liquidity rather than solvency. Principal was rescheduled and new loans made in order to (a) protect banks' capital, (b) ensure continued inflows of interest, (c) avoid taxpayer bailouts of banks, and (d) give countries breathing space within which to stabilize their economies and return to creditworthiness.

Gradually, as arrears mounted and many countries in Latin America failed to grasp the nettle of economic reform, perceptions changed and some banks began to regard the problem as one of solvency. The turning point was in May 1987 when Citicorp created a $3 billion provision against its $14.8 billion sovereign debt exposure, of which $10.4 billion was to Latin America. This resulted in the biggest quarterly loss in U.S. banking history. Other banks in the United States, Canada, and the United Kingdom rapidly followed suit. By the end of 1987, the nine biggest U.S. money center banks had amassed reserves of $12.9 billion against developing country loans.

The banks emphasized in public that the reserves were not to be confused with write-offs or a willingness to accept less than 100 percent repayment of loans. Sir Kit MacMahon, chief executive of the United Kingdom's Midland Bank, told bankers in London in 1988 that provisions were being created to protect banks against the temporary funding losses that occur when debtor countries interrupt interest service. He argued that they were not a recognition of permanent loss of principal and even invoked the old saw that "countries can't go bust."

All these arguments quickly lost their credibility. The emergence of a secondary market for Latin American and other developing country debt and the readiness of banks to use that market to exit from their exposures at a sizeable discount belied the banks' arguments about 100 percent recoverability. Banks employed some of their reserves to eliminate exposure to Latin America. Although bankers resisted giving legitimacy to the secondary market in their public pronouncements, which dwelt on the thinness and fickleness of the market and the insensitivity of secondary market prices to "fundamentals," in practice, banks often used the market to exit from their exposures for cash. Supply onto the market was such that, in 1987 alone, the Shearson Lehman Brothers Developing Country Debt Index, a weighted average value of the debts of twelve developing countries, of which eight are from Latin America, fell by 28 percent from 66.7 in January 1987 to 47.3 by the end of the year. Publicly available data show that between May 1987 and June 1989, the developing country exposure of Citibank fell by $3.8 billion, Chase Manhattan's by $1.4 billion, Manufacturers Hanover's by $1.2 billion and J.P. Morgan's by $0.9 billion. This was prior to the implementation of the Brady Plan, which involves the official and multilateral sectors using a modest amount of their own resources to catalyze debt forgiveness by the commercial banks. Under the Brady Plan, further losses have been sustained. Write-offs by commercial banks against developing country loans, therefore, have been substantial.

This process has caused most pain in the United States, where losses in Latin America compounded problems in other parts of the banks' portfolios. Commercial banks in the United States had to write off about $60 billion of domestic loans in the second half of the 1980s, as loans to real estate companies and other borrowers turned sour. The scale of the overall problem can be gauged from the fact that, in the entire period 1950 to 1980, the whole of the U.S. banking system wrote off no more than $28 billion of domestic and external loans. The Federal Deposit Insurance Corporation, which guarantees bank deposits up to $100,000, lost over $5 billion in 1988 and 1989, when 428 banks failed, the worst performance since the Great Depression.

Yet the United States has not been alone in finding problems in Latin America coinciding with a range of other difficulties. As the 1990s began, the United Kingdom's biggest clearing bank, National Westminster, lost its AAA bond rating. The rating agency cited the erosion of the bank's capital and reserve base, which was part and parcel of its attempts to work down its exposure to Latin America and other developing countries. Of the United Kingdom clearers, National Westminster has been among the most pessimistic about the recoverability of Latin American loans and used its debt-trading team to sell debt for cash, eschewing other means of reducing its loan book, such as debt-for-equity conversion. This process has left it more vulnerable to losses and poor performance in other areas of its portfolio. Domestic portfolio problems mounted toward the end of the 1980s, as the U.K. government's high interest-rate policy subjected borrowers to considerable discomforture, particularly those with high leverage. Among the "big four" clearing banks, Midland saw its stock prices plummet in the 1980s owing, at least in part, to losses incurred on Latin American debt, much of which was taken on to Midland's books in the process of acquiring the U.S. bank, Crocker.

In Japan, a number of large banks, including Fuji and Dai-Ichi Kangyo, have, like National Westminster, been downgraded by the bond-rating agencies. Reverses in the Japanese equity market and the widespread realization that the property market was over-inflated raised doubts about loans collateralized by equities and property. Analysis of the balance sheets of various Japanese money center banks has cast doubt on their ability to bring capital and reserves up to the minimum levels of the Basle (Bank of International Settlements, or BIS) accord, under which banking supervisors have agreed to ensure that banks throughout the world bring capital and reserve levels up to a certain minimum level by 1992. The Basle accord allows Japanese banks to record 50 percent of "hidden reserves"—basically, the unrecorded difference between cost and market valuation of banks' equity and property investments—as "capital." However, the scale of the reserves has been reduced by the weakening in equity and property markets. Given that Japanese banks have not created developing country provisions at the higher levels seen elsewhere in the world, their "hidden reserves" are in a sense also earmarked for losses they will have to sustain in Latin America and other developing countries: to date, stronger Japanese banks have been discouraged by the Japanese Ministry of Finance from selling their debts onto the secondary market, for fear that prices would be pushed further down, bringing into plainer relief the fragility of some less strong Japanese banks with large developing-country portfolios. Calculations undertaken by ICBA show that the falling stock market has pushed down the average ratio of capital-to-risk weighted assets of the twelve biggest Japanese commercial banks to only 7.7 percent, below the 8-percent floor established by the Basle agreement.

Given these adverse experiences in the United States, U.K., and Japanese banking communities, it would perhaps be surprising if banks were to resume lending to, and other commercial contacts with, Latin America in the 1990s. It is not easy to imagine bank managements persuading credit committees and shareholders that loans should be extended to countries that, in the previous decade, have involved banks in losses of a staggering magnitude. Yet, as this chapter will go on to show, Latin America in the 1990s will not be a "no-go area" for commercial banks. This is not to say that the 1990s will in any sense see a repeat of the 1970s lending boom: the next section analyzes the reasons and motivations for banks' involvement in

Latin America in the 1970s, and the section after highlights the big differences between the 1970s and 1990s, both "macro" and "micro." However,
the chapter will go on to argue that there are old and new motivations for
banks to "rediscover" Latin America in the 1990s and for Latin America to
welcome and encourage this rediscovery.

LATIN AMERICA AND THE BANKS IN THE 1970s

The 1970s saw a rapid insertion of Latin America into the international capital markets. In 1970, Latin America had $15 billion of long-term loans from
foreign commercial banks. By 1980, this figure had increased to $120 bil-
lion, representing an eightfold rise in only one decade. By the start of the
1980s, the nine U.S. money-center banks had exposure to Argentina equivalent to 21 percent of their capital, 46 percent in the case of Brazil and 50
percent in the case of Mexico. Thus, these three countries alone had the potential to wipe out entirely the whole of the capital of the U.S. money-center banks. Banks elsewhere in the world, in particular the United Kingdom,
were similarly exposed to massive loss of capital in the event of Latin
America reneging on its debts.

Why banks were willing to expose their capital to Latin American risk on
such a huge scale is a complex story. However, it is worth considering at least
some of the reasons for the banks' behavior to see whether any of their motives
for channeling loans to Latin America have any relevance to the 1990s.

Of the many challenges facing the banks in the 1990s, three were, at least in
retrospect, of particular significance: the rapid pace of financial innovation; the
relative abundance in the aggregate of global savings; and the perverse allocation
of global savings, whereby terms of trade changes favored countries with low
resource-absorption capabilities. These three features of the 1970s were closely
linked. The main product of the process of financial innovation was the Euro-
currency market, a basically unregulated market that allowed commercial banks
a much greater role in cross-border financial intermediation. The relative abundance of global savings—the ratio of savings to GDP in the OECD (Organization
for Economic Cooperation and Development) countries was 24 percent in the
1970s, compared with 20 percent in the 1980s—meant that the OECD loan
market was rather overcrowded, especially when economic recession hit the
industrial countries in the early 1970s. OECD countries include most of Western
Europe, Turkey, Japan, Australia, and New Zealand. The upshot of this was
that banks increasingly looked to cross-border opportunity for intermediation.
In the wake of the two oil shocks, the most obvious cross-border opportunity
arose from the coincidence of excess savings in OPEC (Organization of Petroleum
Exporting Countries) and shortages of resources in the nonoil developing world,
particularly Latin America.

The rather small part played by the multilateral sector in recycling OPEC
surpluses left a vacuum for the commercial banks to fill. They gladly ac-

cepted the recycling role. Although there remain differing views on the extent to which governments actively encouraged banks to undertake this recycling, what is clear is that, during the 1970s, banking regulators in general attached no greater capital weights to Latin American sovereign loans than to equivalent loans to the OECD countries. This discouraged banks from rationing the capital they allocated to Latin American risks. In the 1970s, and at the risk of simplification, it may be said that the preoccupation of bank regulators was to ensure that banks diversified their exposures. They were far less concerned, albeit not unconcerned, about "risk-weighting" exposures or about raising overall capital/asset ratios.

There were other factors behind banks' willingness to lend to latin America, not least of which was the good risk/yield perception of the region. In the early 1970s, the U.S. money-center banks were able to fund themselves at between 0.125 and 0.25 below LIBID (London interbank bid rate). Many of the loans to Latin America were at over 1 percent above LIBOR (London interbank offer rate). Loans also contained a fee structure, with front-end and other fees often reaching 1.5 percent and more of the value of the loan. Fees were frequently used for cosmetic purposes: countries preferred to be seen borrowing at a low spread over LIBOR and pay a risk premium to lenders as a fee. The bid U.S. banks who led the way in the new market found the fee-adjusted yield on the loans attractive. Latin America was seen as a good risk, as the region had grown strongly since the Second World War and had close ties, both commercial and political, with the United States. It was felt that, for example, Mexico was protected from the elements of the international economic environment by a U.S. umbrella, as Mexico's geopolitical importance to the northern country was substantial. On the broader "country-risk" front, banks also observed rising commodity prices in the 1970s. Increases in export prices helped export revenues to multiply as quickly as long-term debt: indeed, the ratio of Latin America's long-term debt to its exports of goods and services was lower in 1980 (139 percent) than in 1970 (149 percent).

In the second half of the 1970s, as U.S. regional and non-U.S. banks began to take a larger share of loan syndications, spreads and fees fell somewhat in the rush to lend. Balance-sheet expansion was very much a part of the banking culture in the 1970s: the increased supply of loans to Latin America inevitably reduced the price. The decline in interest spreads was also encouraged by the shortening of the term of bank loans at the turn of the decade, as banks began to exhibit a degree of nervousness about the impact of the second oil shock on the payments capacity of some developing countries. Banks preferred to make shorter-term loans and forgo spreads. This was part and parcel of the "short-leash" theory espoused by banks. This theory had it that the greater the amount of short-term finance owed by a country, the greater the pressure on that country to do the needful to ensure that it could turn over its lines.

THE 1970S AND 1990S CONTRASTED

This digression on relations between Latin America and the international banks in the 1970s highlights a number of the reasons why banks accepted such a large level of Latin American loans onto their books. It draws out the importance of the global savings and regulatory environment, as well as yield and risk considerations.

In comparing the 1970s and 1990s, the differences stand out more clearly than the similarities. Four differences that are of themselves unfavorable to Latin America's relations with the international banks are especially significant.

First, the *quantity of global savings* at the beginning of the 1990s is lower, in relation to world output, than in the 1970s. This has meant that demand for credit has outstripped supply, forcing up real interest rates. High real returns on loans within the OECD, along with disappointing incursions into international banking in earlier periods, have led a number of banks to domesticate their portfolios, concentrating on home markets. U.S. regional and superregional banks have now exited entirely from cross-border operations. Elsewhere, a conspicuous departee from international banking in general, and Latin America in particular, is Lloyds, the U.K. bank. Having been an important lender to Latin America in the 1970s and having a long-standing involvement in Latin America's domestic banking system, Lloyds has now turned its back on most international activities. In 1990, it announced its willingness to sell many of its Latin American operations and in effect cut its links with the region. As many banks have discovered, high real loan rates at home bring with them automatic capitalization (i.e., a real return on capital employed), facilitating the process of raising capital and reserves to Basle accord levels.

Second, the *distribution of the supply and demand for global savings* is not helpful to Latin America. In the 1990s, the two main sources of savings in the OECD—Japan and Germany—will be to an extent deployed in financing the United States' twin deficits (the national budget and external debt) and the development needs of Eastern Europe. The fourth oil shock is again producing windfall benefits to OPEC members, but a number of OPEC countries now have their own development agendas, which will reduce the extent to which their new surpluses will be available for recycling to nonoil developing countries. Thus, Iran will use its windfall to rebuild its infrastructure after the damage inflicted during the Iran/Iraq war. Saudi Arabia's windfall will be used on building up its military establishment, paying for Operation Desert Storm and assisting those countries, like Turkey, Egypt, Syria, and Morocco, that came to its side after the Iraqi invasion of Kuwait in August 1990. Other countries in OPEC also have substantial absorption potential. There is a widespread need to invest in oil exploration and refining, both of which suffered in the wake of the third oil shock of 1986, when oil prices collapsed and the balance of payments current accounts of many oil-exporting countries markedly deteriorated.

Third, the *banking regulatory framework* has tightened. Banks are being obliged to increase capital/asset ratios. This militates against rapid expansion of loan books. Also, capital requirements are heavily differentiated, with weightings for non-OECD credits considerably larger than weights for OECD credits: this is further encouraging the domestication process referred to in the previous paragraph. In most banking regulatory regimes, new loans to developing countries require specific reserves. For example, in the 1989/ 90 "Brady Package" for Mexico, U.K. banks were deterred from lending new money because of the Bank of England required that they provide at 35 percent both an outstanding principal and new loans. In effect, the Bank of England encouraged U.K. banks to forgive (rather than increase) debt by accepting bonds issued by Mexico at a 35 percent discount to face value of existing debt. The Bank of England stipified that no provisions need be applied to these instruments.

Fourth, banks have been through the *educative process of the 1980s*. In the 1970s, sovereign defaults had not occurred on any scale for more than two decades and those defaults had been on bonds rather than loans, which in the 1970s were a relatively small source of finance for developing countries. Moreover, the 1950s and 1960s had seen the growing importance of multilateral institutions, in particular the International Monetary Fund (IMF), whose remit was seen by the banks as being to protect loan contracts between countries. The multilateral institutions, therefore, offered background comfort to the international banking system. Naive assessments of the impossibility of sovereign states going bankrupt are now no longer common. The reschedulings, moratoria, and arrears that were the stuff of Latin America in the 1980s have taught the banks painful lessons in the science of country risk analysis. Under the Brady initiative, multilateral institutions are sometimes perceived by banks to be egging on countries to renege on loan contracts: the IMF is now willing to disburse to countries in arrears to the banks, a practice the IMF has previously eschewed. In the 1990s, the multilaterals, including the Inter-American Development Bank, are helping to finance debt forgiveness by the banks. Thus, with the losses and lessons of the 1980s and the early 1990s fresh in banks' memories, banks will obviously not be keen to repeat them in the remainder of the decade.

These differences between the 1970s and 1990s can be summarized as follows: banks are bound to be more hesitant in their relations with Latin America, given the recent experience of large losses. The global savings environment has deteriorated, both in terms of the level of savings, as well as the distribution of the supply of and demand for savings, and banking regulators are making it more difficult to lend fresh money to developing countries.

These factors hardly seem ideally conducive to a reentry of Latin America into the international financial system. However, other factors are at play that could lead to such a reentry. This reentry, though, may take a rather different form to that taken in the 1970s. These differences are related to changes in the economic structure of Latin America and innovation in the world's financial markets.

CHANGE AND INNOVATION IN THE 1990s

Economic Reform and Macroeconomic Stability

Latin America is now a very different prospect from the 1970s. Although performance and attitudes vary considerably between countries in the region, it is fair to say that most countries have made serious endeavors to address the long-standing policy errors that contributed to the debt crisis of the 1980s and prevented the early emergence of the region from that crisis.

In the 1970s, Latin America inserted itself into the international financial system more deeply than it did into the world trading system. Although, as is argued earlier, export revenues rose in the 1970s as quickly as long-term debt, stabilizing the ratio of long-term debt to exports, export revenue growth was more often than not explained by higher prices than higher export volumes. Also, as Latin America's short-term debt rose from negligible levels to $68 billion by 1980, the overall debt/exports ratio went up steeply. In the 1970s, particularly in the second half of the decade, loans by banks substituted for, rather than supplemented, domestic savings. They helped "pay" for capital flight and bolstered uncompetitive exchange rates. The tradeables sector was penalized by these policies, which were export-adverse. Consequently, industries producing tradeable goods sought subsidies from government, either directly—cheap domestic credit—or indirectly—by means of quantitative import barriers and high tariff walls. Ultimately, then, banks helped to finance these bad policies, which retarded domestic savings growth and precluded the transformation of the countries of Latin America into export-oriented economies akin to the newly industrialized countries of the Pacific Basin.

As the 1990s commence, many countries in Latin America are earnestly adopting orthodox economic policies and removing supply-side barriers to growth. In *Mexico*, for example, the government has addressed the country's previously chronic fiscal problems and has vastly reduced barriers to trade. Mexico is now one of the most open developing economies in the world. The country has joined the General Agreement on Tariffs and Trade (GATT), having refused to join in the 1970s because of worries about the domestic political fallout. *Venezuela*, too, has applied to GATT for membership. The February 1989 economic program introduced by President Carlos Andrés Peréz freed up and unified the foreign-exchange market and numerous trade barriers were brought down. Like Mexico, prohibitive foreign-investment regulations have been pruned. *Chile* has persevered longest with a tough macroeconomic policy and an open trading system: these basic policies have not been disturbed by the transfer to democratic government in March 1990. In *Argentina*, the government of Carlos Menem has pledged to eliminate the public-sector deficit. Although success on this front has not been complete, Argentina has transformed its trade and exchange regimes and, most significantly, embarked on a privatization program that few thought possible in a country as "etatiste" as Argentina. *Brazil*, too, began in 1990 to grapple with its macroeconomic disequilibria and to pull down protectionist barriers. Price controls are now virtually non-existent and indexation is terminated.

The Debt Overhang

These policy developments do not, of themselves, make Latin America credit-worthy. Latin America ended the 1980s with a massive debt overhang and substantial arrearages to the commercial banks.

Latin America and the Caribbean: Debt Indicators, 1989

Total external debt ($billion)	434.1
(As % of exports of goods and services)	(297)
Debt to commercial banks ($billion)	195.5
(of which, arrears, $billion)	(13.8)

Source: World Bank, *World Debt Tables 1989–1990: External Debt of Developing Countries* (Washington, D.C.: World Bank, December 1989).

Gradually, though, the problems of the debt overhang and arrears are being addressed. Mexico finally implemented its Brady Package in April 1990. Under it, banks were given the choice of: lending new money, equivalent to 25 percent of base exposure; exchanging debt for thirty-year bonds, carrying a fixed 6.25 percent coupon, with eighteen months of interest and the entirety of principal collateralized with funds supplied by the multilateral agencies and Japan; or exchanging debt for thity-year bonds issued at a 35 percent discount to the face value of the original debt, bearing a floating, market rate of interest, and "en-hanced" as to principal and interest in the same way as the 6.25 percent fixed-interest bond. More recently, Venezuela has hatched a similar deal, albeit that the thirty-year bonds are a little less concessional and a buy-back for cash at 45 cents on the U.S. dollar is also incorporated.

These and other Brady deals in the offing may or may not of themselves "cure" the debt problems of Latin America. Some observers believe, for ex-ample, that Mexico's Brady package did not produce deep enough relief to make Mexico's debt and balance of payments situation sustainable in the medium term. However, the combination of debt reduction, through securitization, and policy changes are deeply significant for Latin America and its relations with the in-ternational banks in the 1990s, for several reasons.

Resource Transfers

The first observation is that, while analysts can debate the theoretical "sustainability" of any given level of external debt, there is bound to be a wide margin of error on any estimate of what level is sustainable. External debt puts a constraint on the balance of payments and on the public-sector accounts. It implies a resource transfer to creditors, through interest payments, that is not only a debit to the balance of payments and to the public-sector balance, but a potential drag on growth and investment. However, one of the lessons of the 1980s was that some countries with substantial net external resource transfers—notably, Chile—generated high growth and low inflation, while other countries that stopped servicing their debts—including Argentina, Brazil, and Peru—generated zero to negative growth and hyperinflation. The logical conclusion from this is that countries that stick closest to the imperatives of economic reform and adjustment can handle a higher level of debt than those that do not. The relevance of this for the relations between banks and Latin America in the 1990s is that banks may be, ceteris paribus, prepared to lend money to countries whose debt ratios are (post-Brady) somewhat above the levels with which they would otherwise be comfortable: this provided, of course, that domestic policies are optimal. Already, Chile and Mexico are tapping the voluntary markets for not insignificant sums, even though their debt ratios are higher than conventional country risk analysis would deem safe. Other countries could presumably also in due course emulate Chile and Mexico. Banks will need to be reassured, of course, that countries do not again use the availability of additional finance to dilute economic-reform programs and, ultimately, the quality of the new credits.

Securitization

Apart from the issues of the quantity of debt reduction, the quality or method of debt reduction is extemely significant. The process of securitization that has taken place as part and parcel of the Brady Plan has helped banks. In the 1970s, most of Latin America ignored the bond markets, as bonds by their nature contain more onerous contractual commitments for borrowers than do syndicated loans. In the 1990s, restructured debt is being converted into either registered or bearer bonds. A number of primary issues have also taken place in Latin America in 1990, particularly by state-run oil companies, such as Petroleos de Mexico and Petroleos de Venezuela.

Although bonds, unlike restructured debt, have to be marked to market in many banking jurisdictions in the world, making them less attractive for poorly reserved banks, an advantage of bonds is that they are more easily marketable than restructured loans. This makes bonds more attractive for banks to hold and gives them a commodity in which they can take positions as part of a trading portfolio and place, for fees, with the investor fraternity (i.e., insurance funds). Bearer instruments in particular are harder to renegotiate than restructured debt.

No large Latin American country has defaulted on its bonds in recent years. When Brazil issued "exit" and "new money" bonds in its external debt agreement in 1988, both types of bonds were eventually rated by the bond rating agencies and put toward the top of the "investor-grade" category. The extension of securitization—one of the most important financial innovations of the 1980s—to external debt in the 1990s offers banks the opportunity to manage their Latin American risk more actively.

Market Mechanisms of Debt Reduction

One often forgotten element of the Brady Plan is that it supports two forms of debt reduction: centralized and decentralized. The centralized element is the basic exchange of debt for concessional bonds that, in Brady debt packages, are offered as an alternative to, or substitute for, new money.

The decentralized element is in the encouragement Brady packages give to market mechanisms of debt reduction. These market mechanisms, which include debt for equity, domestic currency buybacks, debt-for-debt exchanges, debt-for-nature swaps, and the like have gathered momentum in the run-up to the Brady Plan. In the 1980s, about $35 billion of Latin America's external debt was retired through voluntary market debt reduction. The three main beneficiaries were Chile, Brazil, and Mexico. Since 1985, Chile has operated two main debt-conversion schemes—the Chapter 18 and Chapter 19 programs—that respectively allow debt to be prepaid at a discount and converted into equity. The country has also had two small direct cash auctions of the central bank debt. Brazil has used debt/equity to a lesser extent than Chile, but has at various stages either encouraged or turned a blind eye to informal conversions and buybacks of government debt by parastatal corporations. Mexico terminated its debt/equity program in 1987, as concerns rose about the possible inflationary impact of the peso creation inherent in the scheme. However, it continued to allow "ad hoc" conversions, including the use of debt in privatizations, such as Mexicana de Cobre. Other debt-reduction measures included, in 1988, an offer to the market via J.P. Morgan for the exchange of debt at a discount for floating rate bonds due in 2008, with U.S. Treasury collateral for the principal.

The Brady Plan was not intended to substitute centralized for decentralized debt reduction, but to encourage further use of market mechanisms. In the first big Brady package, Mexico agreed to reinstate a formal debt-for-equity conversion program whereby $3.5 billion of debt would be accepted at auction for conversion into investment in privatized companies and infrastructure projects. Likewise, the Venezuela Brady package incorporates targets for debt-for-equity conversion to which the Venezuelans are contractually committed. Moreover, the terms of Brady packages agreed or implemented to date reduce the barriers to market debt reduction that existed in rescheduling documentation via the "sharing" and "negative-pledge" clauses, which effectively debarred countries from prepaying their debts at discounts without negotiating cumbersome waivers from all creditors of the relevant clauses in the rescheduling agreements. Brady packages address these problems and give countries greater leeway to negotiate debt reduction with the market without having to secure agreement from all creditors.

The implications of Brady's promotion of market debt reduction for the banks are numerous. To begin with, it allows banks who so wish to substitute their debt for equity investments should they feel that the latter offer a superior or speedier return potential. A number of banks have, for example, already created debt-conversion funds in Brazil whereby debt will be converted into shares in privatized companies. Debt for equity also allows banks to support any customers who wish to take investment stakes in Latin America, which allows banks to create fee income from the process. Buybacks and other market mechanisms will permit countries to have, as it were, a "second dip" at solving their debt problems, should they feel that Brady packages have not gone far enough. This will afford banks who are pessimistic about their Latin American credits the opportunity to exit, improving the quality of residual credits held by more optimistic banks. Market debt reduction also creates demand in the secondary market, which will help prolong the deepening of the market that is already underway. This, in turn, makes the securitization process more substantive, furthering opportunities for active management of Latin American portfolios.

Private-Sector Risk

In contrast to the 1970s, the 1990s look set to become the decade of the private sector in Latin America. During the 1970s, banks tended to abide by the maxim that the quality of credits within a country could never be superior to the credit quality of the country itself. In a superficial sense, this remains true: a good private-sector company can only repay its foreign debts if it can have access to foreign exchange, which has, in general, in Latin America been under the control of the central bank. In the 1970s, many banks refused to lend to the private sector for this reason, preferring to extend sovereign loans. However, with a number of countries now freeing up their foreign-exchange markets or liberalizing foreign-exchange regimes, private-sector risk is becoming more palatable. In many countries in Latin America, private-sector companies had generally not, for a variety of reasons, tapped the voluntary international capital markets on a large scale. This was the case in Brazil. In countries where significant amount of private-sector loans had been incurred—such as in Mexico—corporate workouts took place in the 1980s, with private debtors availing themselves with more alacrity than sovereign debtors of the discounts they could achieve in negotiations with creditors. Indeed, in the early days of the secondary debt market, many creditors swapped out of private debt and into sovereign for the greater protection against short-term losses that this would offer.

In retrospect, most banks that undertook private-to-sovereign swaps now regret having done so, as private-sector workout discounts were lower than those applied in most Brady packages. As the 1990s begin, many previously overindebted private-sector entities are relatively free of their old debt and are taking on new loans to finance domestic and external expansion. Because of securitization (as referred to before) foreign banks are able to sell, as well as hold, such issues. Greater use of put options enable banks that hold private risk to lay off some of that risk and, thereby, reduce the amount of capital needed to back the loan.

Supporting Multinational Customers

Improvements in Latin American economic policy making are designed not only to raise domestic savings, but to open up Latin America to greater foreign involvement. In particular, foreign-investment codes are being liberalized, complementing the wider liberalization of domestic financial markets and trade and exchange regimes. According to estimates made by the U.S. Department of Commerce, the rate of return on U.S. direct investment in Latin America broadly doubled in the second half of the 1980s, albeit to levels substantially below developing economies elsewhere in the world. Improvements in the rate of return, a better business environment, the easing of restrictions, encouragement of debt for equity all augur well for foreign investment in the 1990s. The Institute for International Finance projects total foreign direct investment in Latin America to rise by $9 billion in 1990 and $8.9 billion in 1991, substantially higher than in the 1970s and 1980s.[1] Foreign investment is, of itself, a desirable form of financing developing countries. Latin America itself made considerable use of foreign direct investment prior to the 1970s OPEC recycling wave. The advantages of foreign investment are that it helps to transfer technology and managerial skills; it provides hosts with access to export markets; returns to investors are performance-linked and not directly connected with the vicissitudes of international interest rates; and it is in keeping with the desire to focus future development strategies on the private sector.

However, foreign direct investment should not be seen as a substitute for foreign bank finance. Multinational companies will frequently turn to their banks for loan capital in support of projects, as well as trade finance with which to purchase capital and other inputs. In effect, therefore, multinational corporations can act as a conduit for directing international capital flows to Latin America. The launching by President George Bush in 1990 of his "Enterprise of the Americas Initiative" paves the way, not just for the emergence of a U.S. dollar trading bloc, but a much greater degree of U.S. multinational direct investment in Latin America.

Supporting Economic Change

In development theory, the role of foreign banks is largely confined to the part they play in bridging the investment/savings gap of developing countries. In other words, banks are regarded as intermediaries for channeling savings from surplus to deficit countries. In Latin America in the 1990s, however, many foreign banks will evolve a different, albeit complementary, role in supporting economic change.

The development agenda for Latin America remains very long and complex indeed. Structural reform programs engaged in by many countries involve a massive retreat by the state from financial and "real" economic activities. The most visible element of such programs is the liberalization of the financial system and general capital market reforms. In all of these areas, foreign banks are already participating, sometimes as consultants, but often as stake takers. The U.S. money-center banks have, for example, been eager to exchange their loans for shares in Argentine telephone companies. The deepening of financial systems in developing countries often induces initially negative effects on companies that have overborrowed from domestic banks: these companies frequently find that loans are called in sooner if financial restructuring takes place than if the banking system is left at peace. This in turn can generate more business for foreign banks, be it in the form of "mergers and acquisitions" or corporate restructurings. Financial liberalization also enables foreign investment and commercial banks to apply techniques developed in more mature financial markets. In the first nine months of 1990, Mexican firms alone raised $1.5 billion in debt offerings, secured by credit cards, electricity, telecommunications and other receivables. In due course, mortgages will be securitized in Latin America. Banks will have to help supply a good deal of the financial products that will be demanded by private-sector Latin American pension funds, which are an already growing part of the Latin American financial scene.

All in all, financial and economic reforms offer foreign banks substantial investment banking fee-income potential. According to a survey undertaken by the Office of the Comptroller of the Currency, U.S. commercial banks were already generating substantial fee income from Latin America. In the period covered by the survey (1986–1988), U.S. commercial banks earned income of $251 million from securities and merchant banking activities in Latin America. This was significantly more than was earned in Canada and Europe ($203 million). Although the figures for Latin America are inflated by fees earned from syndicating relendings of external debt—as activity that is now virtually redundant given the move to securitization—the variety of other investment banking opportunities will at least compensate for loss of relending income. Latin America gains from the expertise offered by foreign banks. Also, competition between foreign banks for the investment banking business will frequently involve foreign banks having to enter deals with new finance, especially in corporate restructurings.

Conclusions and Summary

In the 1980s, difficulties arising from the Latin American portfolios of banks compounded the problems faced by banks in other parts of their loan books.

Banks in many parts of the world, particularly in the United States and United Kingdom, have commenced the 1990s with low equity prices. The same banks are finding it problematic in meeting the capital/asset ratios stipulated in the Basle Accord, a problem shared by Japanese banks. There is growing talk, especially in the United States, of mergers and takeovers involving the same money-center banks that were at the forefront of the Latin American lending binge of the 1970s. The losses being inflicted on banks, be they as the corollary of Brady packages or the result of protracted arrearages by Latin American borrowers, make Latin America, at least prima facie, an unlikely candidate for banks' attentions in the 1990s. As the 1990s begin, many banks regard Eastern Europe as holding far more promise for international business than Latin America. As multinational corporations enter Eastern European markets, they will seek support from their banks to finance this expansion. German banks are intimately involved in the process of cementing the unification of Germany, as well as cooperating with their customers who are expanding into Eastern Europe.

Despite these developments, Latin America will probably not find itself beyond the pale of the international banking system in the 1990s, although the story will vary between countries. Those countries that put their debt problems behind them through a combination of Brady Plan relief and sensible policies can expect to return in some way to voluntary markets. Chile, which has dealt with its debt problems through market debt reduction, has so far raised two voluntary loans in 1990 and has arranged in principle a $320-million bond with its main creditor banks. Where countries remain encumbered by a high debt burden post-Brady, Brady restructuring packages pave the way for further market mechanisms of debt reduction.

In general, the 1990s will differ from the 1970s in three ways. First, banks will tend to steer clear of balance of payments financing. There will be a greater appetite for private-sector, as opposed to public-sector, risk. This will be in tune with the private-sector policy orientation of the 1990s. Loans in support of multinational ventures in the region, along with trade finance, which will increase pari passu with the trade liberalization process, will also be a feature of the 1990s. Borrowings by Latin American public-sector entities will tend to be in bond form, with banks helping to underwrite issues, but with the intention of on-selling and placing issues with institutions. The rash of bond issues and private placements by Mexican entities in 1989–1990 proves that there is a market for Latin American paper. The fact that some banks are taking this securitized paper into their books suggests that banks are thus stratifying their portfolios, differentiating between these new, primary issues and their stocks of securitized and nonsecuritized Latin American debt.

Second, although (often rather expensive) bank finance will be available for some countries and entities in Latin America, there is little doubt that the amounts may not be large enough, even post-Brady, to reverse the negative resource transfers to creditors in the 1990s. In the 1990s, countries will have to redouble their efforts to raise domestic savings, attract foreign direct investment, and encourage capital flight repatriation. These are superior sources of capital for countries determined to expand their economies by exporting and liberalizing. Countries must do their best to at least stabilize, if not improve, debt ratios in the 1990s. Negative resource transfers, albeit at a lower level than in the 1980s, are probably inevitable and desirable in these circumstances. As this chapter has argued, the 1980s showed no negative correlation between resource transfers, on the one hand, and growth/inflation on the other. In fact, there was a perverse positive correlation, as countries like Chile used self-help to offset the negative pressures of extremely high resource transfers.

A third and final feature of banks' involvement in Latin America in the 1990s will be greater investment banking activity. The reforms taking place in Latin America make it a natural market for foreign banks' investment banking expertise.

There are two outstanding issues to be addressed: to what extent will the rise of Eastern Europe at a time of a continued shortage of world savings and the regulatory weight attached to Latin American loans militate against a rapprochement between the international banks and Latin America? In fact, these problems need not be insuperable. The countries of Eastern Europe often have their own external debt problems and banking regulators will treat new exposures to these countries in the same way as new exposures to Latin America. Thus, to the extent that Latin America and Eastern Europe "compete" for the attention and loans of commercial banks, Eastern Europe holds no advantages—vis-à-vis use of capital—over Latin America. On the wider front, Latin America has a head start over Eastern Europe on economic reform. It also has a long-standing capitalist accounting structure and this, along with other advantages, will continue to attract multinationals to Latin America and, with them, bank loans. There will be no loan bonanza to Latin America, but neither will there be a loan bonanza in Eastern Europe. Latin America will be concentrating in the 1990s on raising domestic savings as the main contributor to higher investment. This effort is already being supplemented by greater foreign investment, capital repatriation, some supportive foreign bank finance, and the application of foreign banks' investment banking expertise. The moderate, but not insubstantial, quantity of bank loans will be only a small fraction of aggregate international banking flows and global savings. There is, therefore, no reason why Latin America should be "crowded out" by Eastern Europe.

NOTES

1. See Institute for International Finance, *Fostering Foreign Direct Investment in Latin America* (Washington, D.C.: Institute for International Finance, July 1990).

6 Social Conditions in Latin America

Uwe Bott and Scott B. MacDonald*

INTRODUCTION

The economic crisis of the 1980s, which caused economic contraction throughout Latin America, was accompanied by a new phase of social awareness at the end of the decade as the effects of the crisis and the consequences of economic adjustment policies became fully visible. Much of what is believed to be a social decline is not documented in official statistics, but comprehended by the experienced visitor to the region. It is not just an impression, but a fact that activities of the so-called informal sector—an aberration of a successful formal economy—have increased. More people are selling goods and services, from handicrafts to prostitution and drugs, on the streets of many Latin American cities than ten to fifteen years ago. An enumeration of these impressions is surely not enough to give testimony to the fact that the majority of the people in Latin America are poorer today than they were only a decade ago. Hence, an attempt will be made in this chapter to collect available data and analyses in order to draw a more complete picture of the extent of impoverishment and what it means for Latin American development in the 1990s.

The first section of this chapter provides a historical review of the involvement of the international community in poverty alleviation. The second section provides a more detailed analysis of the reasons for the crisis in the past decade. The third section will then provide a brief discussion of why Latin America crashed, followed by a section of whatever information was available to describe

*Scott B. MacDonald is an official of the Office of the Comptroller of the Currency and the views expressed in this chapter do not represent those of that organization.

the state of the nations' poor. Finally, the conclusions in the fifth section will assess our options and how we can do more with less, which even under the most optimistic assumptions seems to be the only realistic scenario.

SOCIAL DEVELOPMENT: A GLOBAL VIEW

The concern of the Western-dominated international community with economic development officially began when the World Bank opened its doors for business on June 25, 1946. The first order of business, however, was not really development, but the reconstruction of a wartorn European continent, hence the official name of the institution that was intended to emphasize its priorities as an International Bank for Reconstruction and Development (IBRD).

As much of the productive sector and physical infrastructure in Europe had been destroyed during World War II, the Bank concentrated on the building of railways, roads, power plants, port installations, and communication facilities. Much of that was done in cooperation with or in execution of the U.S. Marshall Plan. It should be noted, however, that Eastern Europe's "reconstruction" was left to the working of the Soviet Union and that the World Bank had little or no say that region. The early work of the IBRD proved to be a tremendous success, as the prosperity of many Western European countries only a decade later were living proof.

During the 1950s, the same model that had been used so successfully in the reconstruction of Western Europe was now being applied to the very similar and yet so different development needs of the so-called Third World. The need for physical infrastructure in the developing countries was just as great as in the past with post-World War II Europe. However, the reason for which these nations were not properly equipped with such infrastructure were radically different. This basic assumption, that is, to project the reconstruction model for Western Europe (and Japan) into the developing countries in the form of a developmental model, might be interpreted as one of the reasons for the many inadequacies of the foreign assistance efforts. Although the physical infrastructure had been destroyed in Europe, this did not affect the existence of societal institutions, financial systems, and the wealth of well-educated and trained though decimated populations. Much of the latter was missing in the developing nations at the beginning of the 1950s and the decision makers of the world erred in believing that supplying the physical infrastructure alone would lift those countries onto a higher level of development. The importance of institution building rather than building of institutions was not understood by what then became known as the development community. It is obvious that this very narrow approach to development completely ignored the relevance of social development and, in fact, widely accepted the trickle-down theory by which the economic benefits would eventually and somewhat automatically reach the poor.

During the 1960s, there was a shift in the perception of social development. For Latin America, this new approach resulted in the creation of the Inter-

American Development Bank (IDB). Although the concepts for such an institution reach as far back as 1890, its creation was triggered by an increasing
unhappiness within the Latin American region with the way the World Bank
had in the Latin view ignored this continent. Latin Americans also disagreed
with the basic assumptions the IBRD had made during the previous decade in
its attempt to foster development. Hence, the IDB eliminated for all practical
purposes the somewhat artificial distinctions between the so-called productive
sector—infrastructural projects—and the so-called nonproductive sector that en-
compassed projects in such areas as education, health, and housing. The fact
that one could not establish a traditional rate of return for those activities had
labeled them nonproductive. For the IDB, the improvement of social conditions
in Latin America was just as much a priority as the building of roads and
hydroelectric projects. As a result, the IDB did pioneering work in water resource
management and sewerage systems as well as in housing and education projects.
The development of human capital was clearly regarded as equal priority to
physical infrastructure. Additionally, the IDB different approach caused the
World Bank to rethink its own views concerning what development in the non-
industrialized world meant.

In the 1970s, it was realized that the high economic growth rates in Latin
America had failed to bring commensurate benefits to the majority of the poor.
As economist Dudley Seers commented in December 1969: "I believe we have
misconceived the nature of the main challenge of the second half of the twentieth
century. This has been seen as achieving an increase in the national incomes of
'developing' countries, formalized in the target of 5 percent growth rate set for
the first development decade."[1]

Additionally, increasing emphasis on the financing of social-sector projects
through international and bilateral donors had also failed to bring the desired
results. Therefore, more of the basic assumptions that used to define development
were questioned. Most importantly, per-capita Gross National Product, or GNP,
as a measure of development was increasingly in doubt: how could GNP per-
capita describe development, if the income distribution of a country was highly
skewed? Thus, new measures were proposed to better express a country's level
of development, such as the Physical Quality of Life (PQLI), a weighted average
of life expectancy at birth, infant mortality, and adult literacy.

Another related issue during the 1970s was the emergence of the so-called
basic human-needs approach. Basic human-needs, as outlined by the Geneva-
based International Labor Office, entailed: "First, they include certain minimum
requirements of a family for private consumption: adequate food, shelter and
clothing are obviously included, as would be certain household equipment and
furniture. Second, they would include essential services provided by and for the
community at large, such as safe drinking water, sanitation, public transport,
and health and educational facilities."[2] This approach found many proponents,
especially as it emphasized such essential requirements as food and housing.

Thus, we arrived in the 1980s with more questions than answers to many of the issues of economic and social development. Moreover, the societies of the Latin American countries also arrived with many imbalances in income distribution, trade, production and consumption patterns, agricultural productivity, the role of the state, and urbanization. Triggered by its external indebtedness caused by the oil shocks and a worldwide recession as well as its underlying structural imbalances, the countries of Latin America fell into their deepest economic crisis since the 1930s. For those who were poor, the fall was particularly hard, since most governments were not able to afford a social net as tight as those in the developed countries to cushion the impact. In fact, many believed that the admittedly modest achievements in poverty alleviation were seriously threatened by the effects of the crisis and the ensuing and indispensable economic adjustment policies.

The decline in Latin America's social structure was evident in the late 1980s in the erosion of health and education services as well as in the worsening condition of communications infrastructure. Scenes of urban and rural poverty, rising levels of street crime, and other images of the economically dispossessed led to another reassessment of development. While many concurred that the nature of the developmental crisis was long-term, there were doubts about the negative impact on the social structure. If stabilization and adjustment programs are expected to be effective in the creation of more competitive economies, does the gutting of education budgets guarantee the trained personnel required to make the economic miracle work? Additionally, does an unhealthy population provide a solid foundation for a national work force? These questions led to demands for ''adjustment with a human face.''[3] In the early 1990s, concern about the social component of the development process appears to have returned, especially as Latin America's leaders come to grips with the need to make long-term structural changes while safeguarding democratic institutions.

WHY DID LATIN AMERICA CRASH?

Although the Latin American debt crisis has been discussed elsewhere at greater length, this section briefly touches upon some of the more topical dimensions that are related to social conditions. During the 1960–1980 period, annual growth in Latin America amounted to 5.8 percent, while population growth averaged 2.5 percent, leaving a net gain of 3.3 percent. This net growth was higher than in any other developing region. This progress was accompanied by measurable achievements in the social sector. Life expectancy increased from 56 years in 1960 to 64 years by the end of the 1970s. Access to potable water also increased substantially, from under 40 percent to two-thirds of an ever-growing population. Furthermore, health delivery systems and nutritional standards improved.

Although domestic overspending and external shocks (i.e., oil shocks) of the 1970s prepared the ground for the region's worst economic crisis since the 1930s, it was the continued neglect of the structural imbalances of the preceding thirty years that explain the depth of the crisis. Hence, Latin America owed $170 billion to foreign creditors in 1980, an amount that increased to a staggering $443 billion by 1987. During the same period, Latin America became a net exporter of capital, putting an enormous strain on the economies in the region. Gross domestic investment, the key to future growth, remained depressed throughout the region during the 1980s, throwing a long shadow into the 1990s and beyond. In fact, investment levels during the 1980s were below 1970s' levels in many countries, and even below 1960s' levels in others.

Latin America's crash ultimately was the by-product of local economic mismanagement compounded by adverse international conditions. The emphasis on an inward-oriented import substitution model or ongoing and augmented dependence on commodity exports left many countries vulnerable to higher imported input costs, which were often paid for by borrowed money. Greed also played its part, with bankers seeking huge profits based on unrealistic rates of return and irresponsible local elites exporting capital to overseas accounts in the Caribbean, North America, and Europe. By August 1982, when the infamous Mexican Weekend took place, the squeezing of capital from Latin America commenced. The expected strength of global economic growth and high commodity prices, on which so many of these loans were based, proved to be a mirage as recession set in and prices fell. Countries and the banks teetered on the edge of the debt crisis. Although the crisis has given way to being a "problem," debt overhang remains an ongoing factor in many Latin American countries in the early 1990s.

THE IMPACT OF THE CRASH

When looking at the immediately quantifiable implications of the external debt crisis on the social sector in Latin America, two measures come to mind: income per capita and government expenditure in the social sector. In terms of income per capita, declining economic growth rates translate into declining per-capita income ratios, a trend that is enforced at the same time in much of Latin America by its high population growth rate. Thus, it was measured that many countries had retrogressed in terms of per-capita income into the 1960s. In the case of Nicaragua, the retrogression went back to 1960. Although the 1980s are often described as the "lost decade" for Latin America, many countries lost more than two decades of their economic and social development in that time span. Table 6.1 provides a rough indicator of the losses for particular countries.

The second quantifiable datum that reflects the impact of the external debt crisis on the social sector is government expenditure in that area. Austerity measures in most Latin American countries in order to lower budget deficits and as part of internationally prescribed adjustment programs have also reduced spending in the social sector in nominal as well as relative terms. In fact, while overall government spending has declined in the 1980s throughout the region, government spending allocated to social services has proportionally declined much faster than the entire budgetary expense. The impact of International Monetary

Table 6.1
Retrogression in Real GDP Per Capita—1985
Levels Compared with Pre-Debt Crisis Performance (1)

Countries	Comparable Year	Number of Years Retrogressed
Nicaragua	1960	25
El Salvador, Venezuela	1964	21
Bolivia, Guyana, Jamaica, Peru	1965	20
Argentina	1967	18
Guatemala	1972	13
Suriname (2)	1975	10
Costa Rica, Uruguay	1976	9
Barbados, Honduras, Trinidad	1977	8
Chile, Ecuador, Haiti	1978	7
Bahamas, Brazil, Mexico, Paraguay, Dominican Republic	1979	6
Panama	1981	4
Colombia	1977	0

Source: Inter-American Development Bank.
(1) GDP per capita measured in 1984 U.S. dollars.
(2) Data available only for the period beginning in 1975.

Fund stabilization and adjustment programs in the early 1980s, in particular, drew criticism for their impact on the poor. As Prime Minister Michael Manley noted in 1982 after being voted out of office in 1980 in the midst of a bitter dispute with the Fund over economic policy and Jamaica's debt problems: "To compound the crisis, however, this social pressure of austerity is applied in a society which probably does not have the kind of social welfare system which can protect its people from the worst initial consequences of the medicine. Therefore, people are hurt in a situation where they enjoy no safety net and for gains which cannot materialize."[4] Table 6.2 demonstrates the reductions in central government budgets for social spending in the 1970s and early 1980s, when many of the most devastating cuts were made.

Table 6.2
Government Expenditures in Health and Education Selected Countries
(as a percentage of total government costs)

Country	Education 1972	Education 1988	Health 1972	Health 1988
Argentina	20.0	6.9	NA	2.1
Bolivia	31.3	18.4	6.3	1.9
Brazil	8.3	4.8	6.7	9.5
Costa Rica	28.3	16.2	3.8	19.3
Chile	14.3	12.0	8.2	6.3
El Salvador	21.4	17.1	10.9	7.1
Mexico	16.4	7.4	4.5	1.1
Panama	20.7	15.6	15.1	16.7
Peru	23.6	15.3	5.5	5.8
Venezuela	18.6	19.6	11.7	10.0

Source: The World Bank.

Another dimension of Latin America's social problems related to the negative impact of the debt crisis is population growth. In the 1965–1980 period, the annual real GDP growth often forged ahead of population expansion. This meant that as long as the economy grew, it was able to absorb a large number of new entrants, hence, maintaining manageable levels of unemployment. For example, Ecuador's population growth rate in the 1965–1980 period was a high 3.1 percent, but the economy grew by an annual rate of 8.7 percent, which was enough to generate employment opportunities and provide a more comprehensive social net in terms of health and education.

In the 1980–1988 period, economic growth failed to keep ahead of population growth, as demonstrated by Table 6.3. The period of protracted recession meant that the growing numbers of entrants into the employment pool found little or no work. In many cases, this led to seeking a livelihood with the so-called informal economy, which includes the cultivation of coca, refining coca paste, and the trafficking of cocaine as well as contraband goods. This situation has helped stimulate a debate about the impact of population growth in Latin America and its impact on the social system. In certain countries, like Colombia, there was an effort to augment family-planning services despite economic difficulties.

THE STATE OF LATIN AMERICA'S PEOPLE
AFTER THE LOST DECADE

In a Fall 1990 issue of *Foreign Policy*, Jamaica's Prime Minister Manley summarized the social impact of the debt crisis on social development:

Table 6.3
Population Growth and Annual GDP
Growth in Selected Latin American Countries
(in percentages)

	Average Growth of Population 1980–1988	Annual GDP Growth 1980–1988
Argentina	1.4	−0.2
Bolivia	2.7	−1.6
Brazil	2.2	2.9
Chile	1.7	1.9
Colombia	2.1	3.4
Costa Rica	2.3	2.4
Ecuador	2.7	2.0
Jamaica	1.5	0.6
Mexico	2.2	0.5
Panama	2.2	2.6
Paraguay	3.2	1.7
Peru	2.2	1.1
Nicaragua	3.4	−0.3
Trinidad & Tobago	1.7	−6.1
Uruguay	0.6	−0.4
Venezuela	2.8	0.9

Source: The World Bank, *World Development Report, 1990* (New York: Oxford University Press, 1990).

The debt crisis has also fueled the explosive growth of the drug trade; in Colombia wealthy and powerful drug cartels have undermined democratic government. When meeting subsistence needs legally seems impossible, the attractiveness of illegal alternatives, such as drug trafficking increases. Inadequate health services and malnutrition retard the development of millions of children around the world, preventing them from becoming productive members of society. Driven by poverty, rural residents abandon their lands and migrate to cities, placing incredible pressure on urban governments trying to provide basic services and frustrating national efforts to achieve self-sufficiency in food supplies.[5]

Manley clearly captures the broad nature of the debt problem and its linkages to the debt crisis. One dimension worth further mention is the failure of the legal economy and the impetus to illicit economic activities. Latin America's economies have developed "parallel," or "informal," economies that function with businesses and vendors of services not officially registered, paying taxes, nor being regulated. According to Peruvian economist Hernando de Soto, the informal economy has evolved because of the failure of the legal economy in providing a necessary outlet for people's capitalistic energies.[6] Legal systems in Latin America, especially in Peru, where he conducted most of his research, have created too much bureaucratic red tape, making it timely and costly to initiate new enterprises. To survive, maintains de Soto, many people turn to creating their businesses without recognition from the state by not going through the many bureaucratic hoops. Precise numbers of the informal economy do not exist, though rough estimates for Argentina indicate that the informal economy could well be two-thirds the size of the legal economy, with marginally lower numbers in Brazil and Peru. What this means for social development is lost revenues to the state in terms of taxes as well as a failure to tap into a dynamic mechanism of self-help that lacks outside linkages.

Beyond declining per-capita incomes and health and education expenditures, accurately depicting the state of Latin America's societies after the lost decade of the 1980s is not an easy task. Although it easy to describe the *favelas* of São Paulo or the return of dengue fever as a serious health problem to Venezuela in 1989, good hard data on a regionwide basis is lacking. What we are left with is data that are not entirely timely and rough estimates related back to what funds have been provided for recording—life expectancy, per-capita income, and literacy.

The Pan American Health Organization conducted a study published in 1984 that reported: "Many countries face sharp increases in the prevalence of malaria. Mortality due to infectious diseases and malnutrition is increasing."[7] In fact, in 1984, 188,851 blood samples taken in Central America proved positive for malaria, twice as many as ten years earlier. Considering that economic conditions worsened in much of that region in the second part of the decade and that the political situation remained unsettled in Nicaragua and El Salvador, it is doubtful that health conditions improved.

Richard Webb came to some grim conclusions in a study on El Salvador. He identified three commonly cited trends: (i) aggregate open and disguised unemployment and underemployment represent 30 to 50 percent of the labor force; (ii) real median and average earnings have dropped by more than 50 percent since 1978; and (iii) the informal sector, which is characterized by less stability and lower wages, has grown steadily relative to the formal sector and now comprises a majority of the employed population.[8] Moreover, "from 1979 to 1985, caloric and protein intake dropped to levels just under minimum daily requirements. . . . Thus, on a national basis, dietary quality and quantity of nutrients available have probably decreased since 1979."[9]

In December 1988, UNICEF reported that at least half a million young children had died during the previous twelve months because of deteriorating living conditions in all developing countries.[10] About one-third of those children were in Latin America. Although we often focus on the poorest countries in the region, like Haiti and El Salvador, when social decline is discussed, it should be noted that the majority of the children cited in the UNICEF study in Latin America died in Argentina, Brazil, Chile, Mexico, and Panama. This is underlined by increasing infant mortality rates in Brazil, for example, which increased from 66/1,000 in 1982 to 74/1,000 in 1984.

The findings of the UNICEF study were later upheld by the outbreak of an epidemic of sarampion in Bolivia, which by the end of October 1990 had killed around twenty people, including eleven children.[11] After a number of deaths in several provinces, the Bolivian Health Ministry declared a state of emergency. The outbreak was discovered in the highland city of Oruro, 240 kilometers south of La Paz, where fifty-seven children were infected. According to Guido Monasterios, the director of La Paz's Sanitary Unity, the rising level of malnutrition and poor living conditions were key factors in the death toll.

Jamaica offers another example of declining social conditions. Statistics demonstrate that a family of five with two wage earners earning minimum wages were able to purchase only 40 percent of a least-cost minimum basket of goods in the mid–1980s. The social issue has clearly been a political factor, helping Michael Manley and the People's National Party win the February 1989 elections. After years of attempted structural adjustment programs under Edward Seaga (1980–1989), debt weariness clearly set in by the 1989 elections. The pressing need to address the social decline was captured by Trevor Boothe in an October 1989 six-month review of the new Manley administration: "Given the fact that expectations exceed the government's capabilities, the challenge for Manley on the socio-economic side is to finance improvements in education, health, housing, and transportation at a pace that will address social needs, maintain his political credibility, and sustain overall economic viability."[12] It is important to emphasize that the difficult balancing act confronting Manley is evident throughout the rest of the Caribbean and South America, especially in the cases of Carlos Menem in Argentina, Alberto Fujimori in Peru and Ferdando Collor de Melo in Brazil.

Overall, the people of Latin America are hit by increasing under- and unemployment, large wage cuts (30 to 50 percent), increasing costs for food and basic services due to reduced government subsidies, and a contraction of health and social services made available by the government. The problem with poverty in Latin America deals in part with external factors, like the debt crisis, and domestic factors, like structural adjustment programs. In the 1990s, Latin America's economic structure is changing, yet one offshoot of that process is a temporary dislocation of employment. Although longer-term projections indicate that more jobs will be provided when economies like Argentina and Brazil round the corner by jettisoning state-dominated plans and adopting free-market-led growth policies, the short-term concerns remain employment loss and declining health conditions.

By the early 1990s, it was estimated that nearly one-fifth of Latin America's population lives in poverty.[13] The majority of those people, some 40 to 50 percent of the total, continue to reside in rural areas. In Brazil, the most recent estimate of poverty in the nation indicated an increase from 1985's level of 40 percent of the total population to about 50 percent, or around 70 million, in mid–1990.[14] These figures raise the issue of what type of strategies should be adopted to regain lost ground in human as well as economic development for the rest of the decade.

CONCLUSION: WHAT CAN BE DONE?

What can be done at a time when domestic and external resources are scarce and are likely to remain so for the foreseeable future? In the short term, those concerned with development in a holistic sense, including social development, should within very well-defined terms consider targeting the poor. This can be accomplished if there is a partial cost recovery from the "better off" and provision of private social services. At the same time, targeting has a problematic side in that how does one define "poor," at a time when much of the middle class in Latin America has lost considerable ground in its social welfare standing?[15] Therefore, in pursuing a targeting program, it should be carefully weighted with either a geographic (like urban slums or the countryside) or issue-specific approach (like immunization).

Two other reforms are needed: instill greater efficiency in local social service administrations and develop some form of progressive tax reform. With the former, waste is often a problem, while a rigorous questioning over the value of a program is often lacking. Simply stated, many social services administrations in Latin America are bureaucratically top-heavy. Paternalism also plays a role: in many cases, services are extended to those that supported the local elected official, while others, without social services, backed the loser.

In terms of tax reform, Latin America's record with taxes is hardly laudatory. In 1990, Colombia's National Tax Director, Fernando Zarama, announced that his countrymen had some $16 to $18 billion offshore that was not being taxed.[16] Colombia is hardly alone in terms of capital that escapes taxation: it is estimated that Argentina has between $30 to $40 billion in capital flight overseas and Venezuela around $30 to $35 billion. Related to this is the question of why the money sits in offshore bank accounts in the Caribbean, North America, or Europe. The answer is that local investment conditions are not attractive. Therefore, the issue of providing a safety net of social services is related to better collection of taxes as well as creating better macroeconomic conditions that attract the return of flight capital or detract from the informal economy.

The role of outside assistance is debatable. Although capital is needed to fund programs, oftentimes, it becomes a matter of throwing money at a problem without solving it. Unfortunately, corruption also plays a hand in the weakening of social programs. This is not to argue that there are programs that are managed by honest individuals.

Although outside assistance is needed and should be tapped, self-help programs have advantages in that the participants have a clearer perception of what is to be done. An example of this is family planning. Latin American countries confront substantial problems with this issue, especially as a large segment of the population of women are reaching the prime years for child bearing. What will be gained from U.S. assistance in this area when the family-planning issue in that North American country became under the Reagan (1980–1988) and Bush

(1988-   ) presidencies dogmatically pronatal? The problem in Latin America is a combination of too many people and a lack of capacity of local economies to provide them with adequate living conditions and employment in the legal economy. How will more people resolve this problem? If outside assistance is to be provided, it should cover sanitation and family planning, which includes birth control, vaccination, or pre- and postnatal care. Considering the ideological anchor that U.S. assistance carries in this area, self-help programs are probably a better approach because they reflect local needs, not the domestic electoral considerations of North American politicians.

On a long-term basis, reform in the social services sector is dependent on government realization that the development of human capital is essential to improving the national well-being. The productive sectors must reach the poor and, in this, community participation is crucial. Social development is justified not only on human and ethical grounds, but on economic grounds, and development in the true meaning of the word is not possible until this most complex and challenging aspect of the development process is successfully tackled. Without social development, Latin America will not be able to compete economically in the world of the 1990s, especially considering the emphasis placed on the ability of a society to assimilate and use new technology. A poorly educated and malnourished population will not provide solid foundations for a better future.

NOTES

1. Dudley Seers, "The Meaning of Development," *International Development Review* (December 1969), p. 2.

2. International Labor Office, *Employment, Growth and Basic Needs: A One-World Problem* (Geneva: International Labor Office, 1976), p. 32.

3. See Giovanni Andrea Cornea, Richard Jolly, and Frances Stewart, *Adjustment with a Human Face: Protecting the Vulnerable and Promoting Growth* (Oxford: Oxford University Press, 1987).

4. Michael Manley, *Jamaica: Struggle in the Periphery* (London: Writers and Readers Limited Cooperative Society, 1982), p. 164.

5. Michael Manley, "Southern Needs," *Foreign Policy*, No. 80 (Fall 1990), p. 46.

6. See Hernando de Soto with E. Ghersi and M. Ghibellini, *El otro sendero: la revolutión informal* (Buenos Aires: Editorial Sudamericana, 1987).

7. See Pan American Health Organization, *Priority Health Needs in Central America and Panama* (Washington, D.C.: Pan American Health Organization, 1984).

8. See Richard Webb, Alain Thery, Ernesto Kritz, and Elaine Karp, *El Salvador: Income, Employment and Social Indicators, Changes over the Decade* (Washington, D.C.: Agency for International Development, International Science and Technology Institute, Inc., January 1986).

9. Ibid.

10. See UNICEF, *The State of the World's Children, Report 1989* (New York: United Nations, 1989).

11. *The Times of the Americas*, October 31, 1990, p. 5.

12. Trevor Boothe, ''Post-Election Report Six-Month Review,'' *CSIS Latin American Election Study Series, The 1989 Jamaican Elections* (October 19, 1989), p. 11.

13. World Bank, *World Bank Development Report 1990* (New York: University Press, 1990), p. 141.

14. Julia Michaels, ''Brazil Squeezed Into Recession,'' *The Christian Science Monitor*, November 15, 1990, p.8.

15. Laura Kelly brings this point out in her study, which was based on field research in Venezuela in 1989. See Laura Kelly, ''Towards a New Rationale for Community Involvement in Rural Development in Venezuela,'' Master's Thesis for Clark University, 1991.

16. *FBIS, Latin America*, October 16, 1990, p. 32.

7 Regulatory Aspects of the Latin American Debt Crisis: Giving Up Laissez-Faire

Uwe Bott*

INTRODUCTION

The infamous debt crisis officially commenced with a phone call from the Mexican Minister of Finance Silva Herzog to then Secretary of the Treasury Donald Regan on August 13, 1982. Herzog allegedly began this telephone conversation by saying: "Mr. Secretary, we have a problem." Subsequently, Herzog informed Regan of Mexico's inability to pay interest due on its debt. "We," as the story was later told, did not just stand for "We, the Mexicans," but rather for "We, the U.S. and Mexico." This call led to a meeting of the top officials of both countries, labeled the Mexican weekend and the subsequent "Mexican rescue," one of many desperate efforts that would follow attempting to restore the financial liquidity of the debtor countries. It is unlikely that either Secretary Regan or Herzog himself fully grasped the meaning of the latter's words. The vicious circle of never-ending debt negotiations had just begun.

The comprehension deficit on part of the key players in the debt game resulted from a lax attitude on behalf of all participants confronted with the complexities of foreign lending/borrowing and the weak regulatory environments that aided such behavior. Borrowing countries' governments had no or insufficient ac-

*Special thanks to Leon Tarrant, Manager of the U.S. Interagency Country Exposure Review Committee for his helpful insights and guidance in writing this chapter. Mr. Bott is an official with Moody's Investors Service. The views expressed in this chapter are, however, solely his views and do not necessarily represent or purport to represent the views of Moody's.

counting of the level of indebtedness of their own agencies as well as the private sectors. The commercial banks, on the other hand, were involved in a fierce fight for turf and had carefully protected their exposure data from other competitors. The market was too lucrative. Hence, few bankers worried about the debt accumulation of some of their best customers. Countries just did not go bankrupt. Between 1979 and 1982, U.S. banks increased their holdings of loans owed by less developed countries (LDCs) from $81.2 to $139.7 billion.[1] Moreover, LDC debt exceeded bank capital for the largest banks and was disproportionately owed by only a few of the developing countries. To make things worse, many loans had been extended to projects in sectors that did not produce an adequate rate of return or with maturities that were not suited to the particular yielding of the operation. Industrialized country governments and their bank regulators ignored many of these inconsistencies by encouraging the recycling of inflation-breeding petrodollars that had swamped their capital markets after the two oil shocks. They also welcomed any opportunity to cut "unpopular" foreign aid, which was increasingly replaced by commercial bank lending.

The shock of 1982 and of the ensuing events that have now spilled over into the next decade awakened all players and forced them to develop more prudent behavior. This was reflected in some peripheral events, like the creation of the International Institute for Finance. The Institute was established by commercial banks to serve as a clearinghouse of information on bank exposure to foreign countries and country credit risk. Other, more fundamental reflexes led to regulatory changes that toughened the rules in both borrowing as well as creditor countries and improved upon the transparency of financial transactions. Although we are far from a resolution of the crisis even nine years later, it would appear that we are in a better position today to assess the depth of the problem. The system is now capable to identify who has lent to whom and under what conditions. This capacity can also be utilized as an early detection system to prevent future crises.

The first test case, in this context, might become Eastern Europe, where overexposure on the lending or borrowing side would now be clearly visible and unhealthy loan portfolios could be readily spotted. With Eastern European debt increasing from some $155 billion in 1988 to more than $165 billion in 1989, there might be rising concern with respect to the liquidity of certain countries of that hemisphere. Reports indicate that U.S. commercial bank exposure has been cautious. Between December 1989 and March of 1990, U.S. banks increased their exposure by a mere $19 million, from $2,739 to $2,758 million.[2] In comparative terms, U.S. commercial banks are owed only 1.8 percent of Eastern Europe's total debt, whereas they account for a whopping 11.5 percent of all financial claims against Latin America. It is this sort of comparison that has been facilitated by the increased openness following the Latin crisis. This allows determination at an earlier stage where the particular weaknesses of bank portfolios lie. For example, within the overall sound portfolio of U.S. commercial banks in Eastern Europe, a rise in exposure of 24 percent to the U.S.S.R. in the first three months of 1990 is worth flagging.[3]

It is also important to realize the adjustment of lending levels and resource flows to the Latin American countries that took place in response to the crisis. This dramatic change is expressed in the statistics on net resource flows and net resource transfers. Net flows are defined as disbursements minus repayments, whereas net transfers equal disbursements minus total debt-service payments including interest. In 1988, net flows of long-term debt to Latin America were roughly 16 percent of what they had been in 1982. While official lenders more or less sustained their flows during that period with various ups and downs in between, private banks reduced their flows to 3.6 percent in 1986 compared to 1982. Increased disbursements since are the result of involuntary lending. More telling than the flows, however, are the statistics on net transfers. In 1983, net transfers of public and publicly guaranteed as well as private nonguaranteed debt to Latin America became negative and have stayed that way since. Between 1983 and 1989, it is estimated that Latin America exported $133 billion to its creditors. Almost $120 billion of that amount went to commercial banks. This means that Latin America had fewer $133 billion available for consumption and investment during that period than it produced.[4]

To deal with the crisis on both ends, new rules and regulations were put in place to govern debt-for-equity conversions, trading on the secondary market, and zero-based coupon bonds, let alone such practices as securitization and the quest for capital adequacy. Most drastic, perhaps, was the shift from strict adherence to loans as contractual arrangements, ultimately demanding full repayment, to actual debt forgiveness. This shift was encouraged by a change in government policies from voluntary lending—under the Baker Plan—to voluntary debt reduction—under the Brady Plan. It is debatable whether either of these policy plans dealt effectively with the debt crisis, that is, led to a reduction of the debt burden in the developing countries to manageable levels without jeopardizing the solvency of domestic banks and avoiding a taxpayer bailout. Yet, the change of perspective is remarkable.

This chapter addresses regulatory aspects of the Latin American debt crisis. It reviews banking regulations in creditor countries, such as the United States, Canada, Western Europe, and Japan, and how they have coped with three major issues: how to deal with debt drag on the balance sheets, the move toward international harmonization of banking regulations as evident in the Basle Committee, and greatly increased competition. The chapter also briefly deals with banking regulations in Latin America, which, in the aftermath of the crisis, underwent profound changes as governments and financial actors grappled with adverse macroeconomic environments characterized by hyperinflation, foreign-exchange shortages, and the laundering of illicit drug money. Latin American supervisory authorities, too, were forced to admit that their framework of prudential regulations were inadequate in dealing with systemic or near systemic bank failures as in the cases of Argentina, Chile, Uruguay, and Colombia.

The regulatory aspects of the Latin American debt crisis are essential if one is to understand the overall financial environment the region has sputtered into in the early 1990s, from the creditor- and debtor-nation perspectives.

TECHNOLOGY AND INTERDEPENDENCE

Regulatory changes that responded to the Latin American debt crisis must be seen against the background of the radical transformations of the international financial markets during the 1980s. The most significant change came with sweeping improvements in technology. As the office was revolutionized by personal computers, fax machines, and mobile phones, the marketplace was globalized and liberalized. Large sums of money could be moved almost instantaneously by electronic wire transfers. Advances in technology also meant that distinctions between markets blurred and financial services trading became a 24-hour-a-day operation. Finally, its consequence was that transactions, legal or otherwise, became more and more difficult to trace.

Throughout the 1980s, new markets in Europe and Asia were opened to competition. Greater numbers of players were brought into the game regionally as well as sectorally, as insurance companies and investment firms also entered into banking activities. The strict U.S. distinction between commercial banks and investment banks as provided through the Glass–Steagall Act is foreign to most European countries and, of course, the domestic restrictions of the United States do not apply in international markets.

While the marketplace became globalized and international competition among creditor countries intensified, the regulatory framework became a new sea of discovery for the banker and the supervisor. And on that new sea, it was soon evident, that the global system was highly interdependent. As Price Waterhouse's Bob Bench noted: "The internationalization of finance over the past twenty years has created a high degree of *interdependence* in today's financial markets. Now events far away can affect an indigenous financial institution almost immediately and market disturbances in one country can be transmitted instantaneously throughout the world."[5]

The increased involvement of bank regulatory authorities in the major developed countries derived from the systemic threat posed by the Latin debt crisis in the early 1980s. As Michael Martinson, Assistant Director at the Federal Reserve Board described: "This involvement comes from the fact that the amount of bank lending to developing countries with debt service difficulties, in relation to the banks' capital funds, was such that it posed significant risks to several large banks and possibly the banking systems in some major countries."[6] Simply stated, bank regulatory authorities entered the Latin debt crisis through their interest in a safe and sound banking system.

The primary concern of bank regulators in the United States, the United Kingdon, Germany, and France, therefore, has not been the future of economic development in borrowing countries, but to guarantee a banking system that preserves the confidence of the public. This is an important distinction to make. All too often key players misunderstand the role of other players, which causes unnecessary strains on the system. Much of the anti-IMF sentiment, to name a similar case, derives primarily from a fundamental misunderstanding of the role of that institution. Distinct from the World Bank, the IMF does not provide development financing, but rather balance of payment support. Consequently, its policy prescriptions tend to be much more narrowly focused.

The interdependence of international financial markets extends to banking regulations, a factor that was vividly demonstrated in the early days of the Latin American debt problem and was reflected in Mr. Herzog's words. Mexico's, Brazil's, and Argentina's declared inabilities to make their payments in the early 1980s raised questions over the solvency of Citibank, J.P. Morgan, and Bank of America. The perceived Latin American liquidity crunch loomed as a prelude to a creditor-country liquidity crunch. Although the decade was a difficult period for creditor-country banks, especially in the United States, the system survived. United States, European, and Japanese banks made it to the 1990s with the developing countries' debt an increasingly secondary concern.

SIMILARITIES AND DIFFERENCES OF NEW CONCEPTS

In addressing the new challenges, the approaches of creditor banking authorities were not always harmonious and substantial differences continue to exist, especially in the areas of tax and accounting rules. The regulatory response of creditor countries was slow, reflecting a lag between macroeconomic and political events, on the one hand, and policy making and implementation, on the other. In the end, they agreed, however, to allow commercial banks to participate in a debt-reduction scheme to amortize the losses over a period of years rather than up front.

In an attempt to eliminate some of the obstacles to the resolution of the debt crisis, regulators are lately being confronted with two separate and sometimes conflicting objectives. On the one hand, they are set out to create a sounder banking system, and on the other hand, they are bound to "reduce regulatory, accounting, and tax impediments to aid [debt] reduction" as U.S. Secretary of the Treasury Brady endorsed in March 1989 in a speech presenting his debt-reduction plan. Although these goals are not necessarily exclusive, they are not always mutually supportive either. Depending upon the policy priorities in a given country, its regulators will prefer differing approaches. In interviews conducted by Stephany Griffith-Jones, European bank regulators argued that "the main concern of bank regulators and supervisors is not to pursue the objective of the Brady Plan, to facilitate debt and interest reduction, but to safeguard the interest of the depositors by defending the solvency of banking institutions."[7]

Regulatory practices of creditor nations, vis-à-vis the Latin American debt problem, disagree most evidently in the countries' reserve-level requirements for commercial banks and their tax policies. Table 7.1 demonstrates the various differences between U.S., Canadian, Japanese, and European regulations. The most evident dividing line between Europe and the rest of the world lies in its favorable attitude to encourage loan-loss provisions in general, and, in particular, through tax deductibility of such provisions. Therefore, European bankers have

Table 7.1
Tax Treatment and Level of Loan-Loss Reserves:
Comparison (mid-1989)

Country	Tax deductibility	Reserve level
U.S. money centers	No*	58%
U.S. Regionals	No*	65%
Japan	1%	15%
Canada	Yes, up to 45%	45%
France	Yes, up to 60%	53%
UK	Up to matrix level	55%**
Germany	Yes	55%
Switzerland	Yes	55%

Source: Jean Bouchet and Jonathan Hay, in Stephany Griffith-Jones, editor, *European Banking Regulations and Third World Debt: The Technical, Political and Institutional Issues* (Brighton, UK: Institute of Development Studies, 1989), p. 7.
*Tax deductibility does apply to so-called Allocated Transfer Risk Reserves, which are mandatory (see what follows), but account for a small portion of all reserves.
**As of September 1990.

been more at ease in establishing loan-loss reserves against their lending to LDCs. Japanese banks have the lowest levels of reserves of all creditor countries. Although some of these low reserve levels were substituted by so-called hidden reserves such as unrealized securities and property gains, there has been an increasing perception of overexposure of Japanese banks to LDC lending.

U.S. banks have increased their loan-reserve levels substantially during the past few years. However, there are two important caveats with respect to that increase. First, U.S. banks have a much higher exposure to LDC lending than the other creditor country banks, whose portfolios, in some cases, are concentrated on other high-risk areas, such as Eastern Europe. Thus, large amounts of risky LDC debt is still not covered by U.S. reserves. Second, according to U.S. law, general reserves may be included in the capital base. That means, if in fact a bank participates in a debt-reduction operation, the recognized loss leads to both a decline in reserves as well as in bank capital without tax benefit, whereas in countries without capital inclusion such operation would only affect the capital base to the extent that the losses exceeded the reserve levels.[8] This leaves U.S. banks much more exposed to the economic fate of its debtors, in spite of the recent increase in reserve levels. It also presents an important obstacle for effective debt reduction.

In turn, it has been the U.S. viewpoint that the tax deductibility of loan-loss reserves, which is common in Europe, presents an obstacle to a successful debt-reduction strategy. As full tax incentives are allowed at the time of provisioning in most European countries, there is no tax incentive to accept actual debt or debt-service reduction. It is important, in this context, to understand that loan-loss reserves do not indicate that a bank surrenders its claim against the asset. It is simply an accounting measure that protects a given bank from counting as assets outstanding loans whose value is so impaired that the likelihood of re-payment is relatively low. Thus, in Europe the tax incentive is given to banks that acknowledge the weakness of some of their claims without surrendering them. It is suggested that European tax policy be such "to ensure that sufficient (but not excessive) levels of provisioning are maintained."[9] Of course, this is an excellent example for the conflict between short-term and long-term interest, between resolving the specific debt crisis and safeguarding the sound-ness of banking. European banks were less vulnerable to potential defaults of their Latin American debtors, because they quickly recognized the problem and reacted to it by increasing their reserve levels. They were encouraged to do so by tax incentives. It can hardly be argued that their interest or that the interest of their depositors would have been better served by provisioning less in the expectation of future debt reductions. Such tax policy change, therefore, is not desirable since it would only serve a short-sighted, yet laudable goal while endangering the systemic advantages of European banking. Prudential banking must remain the overriding objective of banking supervision.

Some of the differences between banks from various creditor nations will be eliminated once the new capital-adequacy guidelines of the Bank for International Settlements (BIS) will be applied by the end of 1992. As there was no inter-national uniformity of banking regulations and because of the liberalization of capital markets during the 1980s in combination with the lingering debt crisis and its effects on the international banking community, BIS felt compelled to develop universal guidelines on key issues. In July 1988, after long negotiations, its Basle Committee agreed upon common standards on such issues as provi-sioning and capital adequacy. Under this agreement, specific reserves are to be excluded from capital. This had been already the case for U.S. banks, but not for French banks. General provisions will be excluded from what is called core capital, that is, equity and disclosed reserves, but may be included in supple-mentary capital up to 1.25 percent of risk-weighed assets. This rule change will indeed affect U.S. banks. A participation in debt-reduction operations will then no longer threaten the capital base of U.S. banks. Finally, capital-adequacy rates were set at 8 percent.

Additional dissimilarities between the policies of creditor regulators, which will not be reconciled by the Basle agreement, also exist with respect to interest-

income accruals. U.S. banks put LDC loans on a nonaccrual basis when arrearages exceed 90 days. U.K. banks continue to accrue the interest in spite of
a delinquency and make specific provisions only when it is perceived that there
is a considerable chance that the interest will not be recovered. Finally, European
and U.S. laws and regulations differ regarding the treatment of interest capitalization. Although U.S. laws discourage capitalizing interest by not including it
in reported profits, yet counting such capitalization as taxable income, their
European counterparts are more flexible. Generally, capitalized interest is not
regarded as income and, therefore, is not taxable.

In summary, there are many regulations in various creditor countries that have
been adjusted during the past decade to deal with the crisis in a more concerted
way. Still, many differences remain in the way in which creditor countries deal
with the impending default of many of their debtors.

IMPLEMENTATION OF THE NEW RULES

Of equal importance to the regulatory framework itself is the way in which these
rules and regulations are being enforced. The most complex of all appears to be
the British matrix. In 1987, the Bank of England developed a scoring system
by which credit risk was to be assessed by relating the recoverability of a loan
to three subdivided categories: (a) evidence of a borrower's inability or unwillingness to meet its obligations; (b) a borrower's current difficulties in meeting
obligations; and (c) factors that evaluate the probability that these difficulties
will not be overcome. In accordance with the results of the scoring matrix,
specific mandatory provisions are set. The British system, while admittedly very
complex, appears to be the most transparent one and excludes subjective factors
from the process as far as this is feasible. German regulatory authorities are
rather noninterventionist. It is left to the banks themselves to decide on the levels
of loan reserves.

U.S. supervisory procedures for commercial banks with foreign lending portfolios are unique and deserve special attention. Responsibility for regulating
commercial banks in the United States is shared by three separate federal agencies: the Office of the Comptroller of the Currency (OCC), for all practical
purposes an independent unit, legally, however, part of the Treasury Department;
the Federal Deposit Insurance Corporation (FDIC); and the Federal Reserve, the
U.S. central bank equivalent. Until 1979, these three agencies evaluated the
foreign exposure risk of domestic U.S. banks independently from each other
and came to, as might be expected, very different results with regard to very
similar country risks. This separation of supervisory responsibility goes back to
1863 when OCC was first established and thereafter to 1913–1914 with the
creation of the Federal Reserve. It is legally documented in the U.S. banking
laws of the 1930s, and is an expression of the U.S. philosophy of controlling a
system via an elaborate web of checks and balances. Although the British system

is complex with regard to the practical application of an elaborate matrix, the U.S. system is particularly complex with respect to its institutional framework.

Supported by a recommendation of the U.S. General Accounting Office (GAO), the regulators of these three agencies decided in 1979 to create a committee called the Interagency Country Exposure Review Committee (ICERC) to assess transfer risk in credits extended by U.S. banks to public and private entities in foreign countries. This process, however, was uncommittal to the banks in the sense that the committee had no authority to demand reserve requirements until the International Lending Supervisory Act was passed in 1983. This law was drafted in the height of international hysteria about the debt crisis and its possible effects on the commercial banks of the creditor countries. It provides explicitly for the three agencies to develop uniform systems of supervision that ensure, among other things, that "banks achieve and maintain specific reserves for foreign loans required by the agencies."[10]

As a result, the three agencies participating in ICERC prepared very specific guidelines by which they conduct their supervisory activities. The process itself is a bit of a secretive operation, best captured by Bruce Stokes in his article on the subject as follows: "Nine men, whose names even the closest reader of *The New York Times* or *The Wall Street Journal* might not recognize, sit locked in a room at the Comptroller of the Currency's office in L'Enfant Plaza in southwest Washington. Laboriously, they sift through bank loan records and economic assessments of debtor countries. After a week of deliberation and some sharp disagreements, their decision will send tremors through the international financial system, cutting the profits of some U.S. banks and impairing the ability of many Third World nations to obtain commercial credit."[11]

Although this process appears more like the meeting of the world's cardinals in search of a new pope, some light can be shed on this secretive exercise. First of all, the secrecy itself, while possibly overdone, has the purpose of ensuring confidentiality of the issues involved. It is not in the interest of borrowers and lenders alike to create an environment of chaos were individual country-risk assessments made by ICERC or the subsequent reserve requirements were publicized, to create a run on the banks that hold assets in those countries targeted. Confidentiality is one of the key ingredients to a prudent banking system.

The composition of ICERC is that of three bank examiners per agency. Their starting point is the assessment and classification of country risk by evaluating the economic, social, and political risk factors. Part of this assessment is based on studies prepared by the Federal Reserve Bank of New York and the Board of Governors of the Federal Reserve. As a next step, the examiners visit U.S. money-center banks to review the countries on the agenda with bank management. They engage in an exchange with the senior officers of those banks on their risk assessment of the respective countries. In a last step, ICERC categorizes country debt according to certain agreed standards and, as a result, recommends additional reserves, called Allocated Transfer Risk Reserves (ATRR), from those banks that have exposure to those countries. The risk assessment does not have to be uniform for a given country, that is to say depending on the nature of the respective debt paper of a given country, this paper may fall into different risk categories.

The categories ICERC uses to rank country risk are the following:

1. Strong: no perceivable problems of repayment.

2. Moderately strong: limited internal problems, but none likely to affect orderly repayment.

3. Weak: problems, which, if not reversed, could threaten future orderly repayments.

4. Other Transfer Risk Problems (OTRP): countries that are not complying with their external debt-service obligations, but are taking positive steps, or countries on the verge of noncompliance. This category also includes countries that have graduated from the categories that follow, however, sustained resumption of orderly debt service needs to be demonstrated.

5. Substandard: countries not complying with debt-service obligations and not pursuing adjustment programs or not negotiating debt rescheduling.

6. Value-impaired: countries with prolonged debt-servicing arrearages, which are not complying with IMF or similar programs and there is no immediate prospect for compliance, or the country has not met rescheduling terms for over a year, or the country shows no definite prospects for an orderly restoration of debt service in the near future.

7. Loss: loans to a given country are regarded as uncollectible and not bankable asset.

The categories of substandard, value-impaired, and loss are defined as classified assets. At present, however, ATRRs are only applied to value-impaired loans. Losses have to be declared as such.

The ICERC meets three times a year and even the dates of these meetings are usually kept in secrecy. After the meeting, which decides by simple majority on the transfer risk of those countries on the agenda, affected banks are contacted directly by their primary U.S. supervisors.

The ICERC also evaluates transfer-risk exposure from a number of other perspectives to obtain a full picture, such as, for example, from the angle of asset concentration. Although high-risk asset concentration does not cause an ATRR requirement, a report prepared by the Committee does makes mention of such cases with heightened risks.

The effectiveness of this very detailed assessment of transfer risk aimed at protecting the interests of depositors in U.S. banks has been criticized from the start. Some bankers have claimed that ICERC does not have the professional expertise to judge the ability and willingness of debtor nations to repay. This charge is without grounds, considering the wealth of sources available to the examiners. Bank examiners have access to insider information not privy to the eyes of commercial bankers. The second criticism targets the political nature of the evaluation process. The interests of the three agencies involved are quite different. The FDIC as the insurer of deposits has a very conservative approach to risk for obvious reasons. The Federal Reserve takes a more global approach in line with its more generally oriented macroeconomic responsibilities. The Office of the Comptroller deals with the issues very professionally, while being sometimes somewhat pressured by the policy interests of the U.S. Treasury Department. The political squabbling sometimes begins with setting the agenda, that is, with the decision on the countries to be reviewed, and ends with the final decision, at times only supported by a slim majority. As one government official was quoted as saying: "Bank supervision is supposed to be an apolitical function, but that doesn't mean people don't put their fingers in the pie."[12]

But, the most important criticism of the ICERC process came from the agency that helped in the creation of the Committee. In a study in 1988, the GAO pointed out that by that year, the ICERC had required only $2.3 billion in reserves for foreign loans, whereas banks themselves had set aside some $21.1 billion, an amount still regarded as inadequate by GAO. Furthermore, the ICERC had failed to: (i) consider country-risk and country-exposure concentrations in assessment of capital adequacy; (ii) examine adequately bank compliance with required reserves; (iii) review the accuracy of banks' country-exposure reports of international loans; (iv) review banks' country-exposure management systems; and (v) comment on assets that are rated weak. Basically, the GAO suggested that ICERC did not do its job as provided in the International Lending Supervision Act of 1983.

There is no doubt, that the ICERC is exposed to political pressures that might not always allow for the best professional judgement. However, the ICERC is a useful instrument. Its partial failure lies in the neglect of the U.S. government to utilize it more effectively within the parameters allowed by the law. In that way, the ICERC might become a proactive contributor to a resolution of the global debt crisis.

The Baker and Brady plans have so far not resulted in substantial reductions of the debt burden on the developing countries or, for that matter, returned these countries to a path of self-sustained growth. Many countries have made considerable efforts from trade liberalization over privatization to domestic austerity programs in order to comply with the prescriptions of international and bilateral donors through various adjustment programs. Yet, eight years after the crisis began, the countries of Latin America have made little progress in attempting to resolve their external indebtedness.

Both the Baker and the Brady plans, which mapped out strategies to decrease the debt burden, were based on one important feature, that is, the voluntary participation of commercial banks in either new lending (Baker Plan) or debt reduction (Brady Plan). Both officials were convinced that the persuasiveness of their arguments would induce such voluntary participation. This, however, has remained a major obstacle to a resolution of the crisis. While the U.S. government rejected the idea of forcing the banks to contribute their share, the banks complied with their responsibility toward their shareholders by not assuming losses that might otherwise be avoided. Consequently, the U.S. government kept its "virginity" with respect to direct intervention and the banks kept their profits, at least on the books. Meanwhile, the debt crisis was allowed to linger. Yet, the U.S. government could keep its "innocence" without remaining passive by utilizing the ICERC process. No laws would need to be changed. All that would be required is the strict application of existing rules. The government would call a spade a spade and expand the list of currently eleven countries whose loans are regarded as value-impaired.[13] Many countries would certainly "qualify" for such classification and have so far been spared for one reason or another, most of which were unrelated to their capacity to repay debt. If the ICERC recognized the value-impaired status of much of the lending to Latin America rather than giving it an almost nonconsequential substandard rating, banks would then be forced to increase their reserves against losses because of the ATRR mechanism. Although this is a costly exercise for the banks since it results in income losses, this effect is cushioned by the tax deduction allowed for such reserves. Hence, the burden of these "losses" are shared by all. By the same token, a rigid application of what is interpreted as value-impaired might steer the banks toward a more active participation in debt-reduction arrangements for damage-limitation purposes.

In conclusion, the regulatory environment in creditor countries has undergone substantial changes during the past decade. These changes have resulted in better supervision and more prudent banking. Commercial banks have over the years improved the composition of their portfolios and reduced their exposure to Latin America either directly or through provisioning. Some of these changes were the results of various schemes, such as swaps and conversions. Some of the debt was simply rolled over from commercial to official lenders. In fact, it can be observed that the crisis brought about a reversal of a trend that was predominant during the 1970s. In 1970, 51.9 percent of all public and publicly guaranteed Latin American long-term debt was owed to official creditors. This percentage shrunk to 20.3 percent in 1983. Official creditors had been replaced by commercial banks who were holding 66.2 percent of all claims. With default lurking around the corner, official creditors picked up the pieces and by 1989 were back at being owed 31.2 percent of the total, while the share of the commercial banks was down by 10 percent.

Still, considerable debt remains. In fact, debt has increased over the years, primarily as a result of accruing interest payments. While there had been a decline of debt stocks for the first time in 1988, 1989 figures show that despite debt-reduction schemes and some outright debt forgiveness, debt will have increased again over the 1988 figures, although not quite reaching 1987 record levels. Also, it must be considered that the Brady debt-reduction modalities reduce the borrowing countries' financial flexibility. Although these mechanisms reduce the debt stock of a given country, they also change the composition of the remaining debt. The bonds that are to replace some of the original debt through the process of rescheduling are regarded as senior debt and cannot be included in future debt-rescheduling negotiations, if they became necessary. It should be remembered that there are historic precedences of Latin American defaults against bonds. Seniority of debt is a convention and will hold just as firmly as the conviction that countries do not go bankrupt. It is clear then that further efforts must be made by regulatory authorities in all creditor countries to provide an environment that will encourage true debt reduction.

LATIN AMERICAN BANKS IN THE 1980s

Providing an overall assessment of Latin American banks in the 1980s is difficult in view of the many differences in regulatory and accounting procedures as well as in light of vast dissimilarities with regard to their level of sophistication and market size. However, some broad-range generalizations can be made, especially in terms of crisis and crisis response.

First and foremost, most Latin American banks did not escape the region's substantial economic problems. Second, many governments found their supervisory policies to be inadequate in coping with a collapsing financial sector. They had failed to create and maintain prudential banks and had not provided enough autonomy for banking supervisory agencies vis-à-vis political influences. A third commonality was that local bank management followed poor lending procedures. Therefore, as Latin America entered the extended period of the debt crisis in the early 1980s, its banks were characterized by inadequate accounting and prudential regulation, compounded by weak supervision.[14]

Some countries experienced what can be described as systemic crises of the banking sectors during that time period. The most severe ones occurred in Argentina, Chile, Colombia, and Uruguay. Systemic crises, in this context, were described as a situation in which "a significant proportion of the banking system became insolvent," with these insolvencies at least partially caused by macroeconomic events.[15]

The Colombian case provides some insight into the mechanics of a near-systemic banking failure. Although Colombia did not reschedule its external debt in the 1980s, the country was hit very hard by the international recession and rising interest rates at the beginning of the decade. The government as well as bankers were not prepared for the rapid slowdown in growth after the coffee boom of 1976–1980. Still, the banking sector appeared healthy in 1981, when in fact Colombian banks had overextended their lending to industrial/financial conglomerates. These inherent problems became evident in 1982 when two of those conglomerates went bankrupt. Both the Banco Nacional and the Banco del Estado were highly leveraged and were unable to avoid the crash of those conglomerates. Consequently, the Banco Nacional was liquidated and the Banco del Estado nationalized. In both cases, deposits were fully covered. However, the failure of two major banks, runs on their deposits, and the revelation of lending to related parties sent shock waves through the country. Hence, a democratization of bank ownership and the role of the superintendency of banks became widely discussed subjects. One outcome of all of this was new legislation

strengthening restrictions upon interlocking ownership of industrial/financial conglomerates, limits on portfolio concentration, and limits on ownership of banks
to 20% of their capital base by any single shareholder."[16]

The Colombian banking system was not out of the troubled waters yet. The
new legislation had passed, but did not have time to become effective, because
the "portfolio of several financial institutions was already too concentrated."[17]
By 1984, Banco de Colombia, the nation's largest private commercial bank, and
the Corporacion Financiera Grancolombia, the leading finance conglomerate,
were threatened by bankruptcy and were subsequently nationalized. This was
followed months later by the government's intervention in the Banco de Bogotá,
Colombia's second largest private commercial bank. Reasons for these failures
stretched from management incompetence, over risky lending operations overseas, to costly takeover battles.

Colombia's banking crisis lasted until 1986. Until then, the superintendency
intervened in twenty financial institutions.[18] Although intervention managed to
prevent financial collapse, the authorities sought to take additional measures to
safeguard the country's financial future. Improvements were made in prudential
regulations and supervision and a Deposit Guarantee Fund (FOGAFIN) was
created in 1985. FOGAFIN's mandate is similar to that of the FDIC in the United
States as it insures deposits for a fee, complements the supervision work carried
out by the superintendency of the banks, and assumes control of ailing institutions
in order to liquidate, recapitalize, or merge them with healthier institutions.

Although problems have persisted in the Colombian banking sector, it was
healthier at the close of the decade than it had been at the beginning. It could
be argued that the debt crisis indirectly provoked a banking crisis that was waiting
to happen. What transpired in Colombia like in so many other Latin American
countries was a regulatory improvement of how to supervise, assess problems,
and react to failures, hence, upgrading the overall banking sector and enhancing
its competitive ability with a rapidly changing international environment.

Still, this is only the beginning of a long and arduous path to establish financial
institutions across the Latin American region that provide the ground for self-
sustained economic development through prudent, efficient, and competitive
banking. The crisis has taught many painful lessons, and many are yet to be
learned.

But there is no need to despair. The financial sector is probably one of the
most complex while crucial elements of the economy. Even most industrialized
countries are still battling with the multiple objectives of prudent, efficient, and
competitive banking. Savings-and-loan institutions have failed in the United
States with breathtaking speed. Their failure was mainly caused by imprudent
banking and lax supervision. U.S. commercial banks have detected inefficiencies
and are laying off personnel while cutting dividends because their portfolios are
often imbalanced with high exposure to LDC, real estate, and farm loans. Finally,
many banks in the smaller, yet prosperous industrialized countries, such as the
Scandinavian countries, have realized that their highly protected financial insti-

tutions are not competitive in an internationalized and globalized financial market of the 1990s. In conclusion, financial institutions in the creditor countries as well as in the countries of Latin America are confronted with many challenges, while the governments in those countries are faced with the task of providing the regulatory environment in which these institutions can function and fulfill their roles in their domestic economies as well as in the international markets.

NOTES

1. United States General Accounting Office, *International Banking: Supervision of Overseas Lending is Inadequate* (Washington, D.C.: GAO, 1988), p. 13.

2. Federal Financial Institutions Examination Council, "Country Exposure Lending Survey," March 1990.

3. Ibid.

4. The World Bank, *World Debt Tables 1989–1990*, Volume 1 (Washington, D.C.: The World Bank, 1989), pp. 95, 96.

5. Bob Bench, *Modernization of Regulation and Supervision of LDC Regulations* (Washington, D.C.: Price Waterhouse, 1990), p. 17.

6. Michael Martinson, "Accounting and Regulatory Policies Affecting Debt Restructuring," in Christine A. Bogdanowicz-Bindert, editor, *Solving the Global debt Crisis: Stategies and Controversies from Key Stakeholders* (New York: Harper & Row, 1989), p. 143.

7. Stephany Griffith-Jones, *European Banking Regulations and Third World Debt: The Technical, Political and Institutional Issues*, Discussion Paper 217, (Washington, D.C.: Institute of Development Studies, 1989), p. 2.

8. The World Bank, *World Debt Tables 1989–1990*, volume 1 (Washington, D.C.: The World Bank, 1989), p. 55.

9. *The Financial Times*, November 22, 1989.

10. United States General Accounting Office, *International Banking, Supervision of Overseas Lending is Inadequate* (Washington D.C.: GAO, May 1988), p. 15.

11. Bruce Stokes, "Mystery Surrounds Agenda, Decisions of Foreign Loan Review Committee," *National Journal* (September 5, 1985), pp. 2136–2139.

12. Ibid., p. 2138.

13. The World Bank, *World debt Tables 1989–1990*, Volume 1 (Washington, D.C.: The World Bank, 1989), p. 54.

14. Felipe Morris, with Mark Dorfman, José Pedro Ortiz, and Maria Claudia Franco, *Latin America's Banking System in the 1980s: A Cross-Country Comparison* (Washington D.C.: The World Bank, 1990), p. xi.

15. Ibid., p. xv.

16. Ibid., p. 90.

17. Ibid.

18. Ibid., p. 91.

8 Global Environment in the 1990s and the Prospects for Latin America

James Thornblade

INTRODUCTION

Whether Latin America will lose another decade in economic development will be determined primarily by its domestic economic policies. That is the fundamental lesson of the debt crisis in the 1980s. However, the global economic environment will also play an important part in determining whether by the year 2000 Latin America will achieve a significantly higher standard of living.

Improved prospects in Latin America require a favorable economic environment in the industrial world, defined as the OECD countries in North America, Europe, Japan, and Australia/New Zealand, as well as the newly industrialized countries of Asia (Korea, Taiwan, Hong Kong, and Singapore). This favorable environment has three dimensions. First, the industrial countries need to sustain their economic growth by means of appropriate monetary and fiscal policies that permit lower real interest rates. Second, the industrial countries must work for a successful outcome to multilateral trade talks (the GATT Uruguay round) that assure an open and expanding system of world trade. Third, industrial countries must direct sufficient external financial resources to Latin America—a major challenge given the collapse of voluntary commercial bank financing to the region.

In addition to a favorable overall global economic environment, the recovery of Latin America will be influenced by three important structural changes. First, rapid changes in the structure of world industry suggest that the future lies with countries that emphasize education and knowledge—intensive industries, with a declining importance for unskilled labor and natural resources. This trend is disturbing for Latin America, which is rich in natural resources, but falls short in human resource development.

Second, while the United States still takes the lead in international economic policy issues, particularly in its historic sphere of influence in Latin America, it no longer has the financial resources to back its policies. Washington increasingly looks to Japan and, to a lesser extent, Europe to provide both official and commercial finance for Latin America. The dynamism of the Pacific Basin is fueled by the world's largest creditor, Japan, and an important question is to what extent Latin America, particularly those countries that border the Pacific, are likely to participate in the Asian economies.

Third, Europe, which historically has played an important role in the development of Latin America, is now preoccupied with the challenge of integrating industrial and less-developed economies within a new greater Europe that stretches from Dublin to Lisbon and Moscow. Prospects for European trade and finance with Latin America are uncertain, given the urgent investment requirements in Eastern Europe, and the likelihood that a vigorous and enlarged Europe may be expected to take the lead in assisting the urgently needed recovery of Africa, Europe's historic sphere of influence.

The remainder of this chapter will discuss these four dimensions in the 1990s and their impact on Latin American prospects, that is, global economic performance, the changing structure of the world economy, the decline of the United States and the rise of Japanese financial leadership, and the emergence of a new greater Europe.

GLOBAL ECONOMIC FORECASTS AND LATIN AMERICA

Latin American economic performance will be even more sensitive to world economic growth rates in the 1990s than in previous decades, because the restructuring of the region's economies is making them more open to the influence of international trade. Import barriers have already come down in Chile as well as, more recently and dramatically, in Mexico. The process of opening up the economies in Argentina, Brazil, and the Andean countries is moving ahead on a more irregular path. This move away from the import-substitution industrialization model requires dynamic and competitive export performance, if the Latin American balance of payments deficits are to remain manageable as import demand is freed to expand. Export performance depends critically on the sustained growth of the world economy and a fair access to international markets.

At this time, the industrialized (OECD) world continues in an expansion of record length that began in the early 1980s. The expansion is due to an unusually smooth transfer of growth leadership from one part of the OECD to another. The expansive policies of the Reagan administration caused the United States to lead in growth in the mid–1980s, but at the expense of enormous deficits in the U.S. budget due to tax cuts and in the external account due to an overheated economy and overvalued dollar. Subsequent efforts to control these deficits, largely through U.S. monetary restraint, did not, however, tip the OECD economies into recession. World expansion was sustained by growth in Japan and other Asian countries as well as in Europe, where investment was stimulated by prospects for the new enlarged market.

Looking ahead into the 1990s, in terms of business-cycle history, one should not be surprised by the recession in 1991. Nevertheless, a case can be made that with the absence of obvious signs of overheating in economic expansion in the OECD countries, the extraordinary opening up of the socialist systems in Eastern Europe, and the continued Asian growth stimulated by intraregional trade, a world recession will be further postponed or mild in magnitude.

There is still, however, the risk that a severe supply shock, such as the withdrawal of oil production, due to the instability in the Middle East, could trigger a world recession. Also, overshadowing the prospects for a continued world economic expansion are the persistent U.S. budget deficit and external imbalances between the major industrial countries. These imbalances cause excessive reliance on monetary policy and volatility in interest rates and exchange rates. Real interest rates have remained high relative to the long-term historic trend, a development that has posed a heavy burden in Latin America, which borrowed on floating-rate commercial terms in the heyday of external finance.

The basic global economic scenario offered by the World Bank assumes that steps will be taken in the OECD countries to reduce fiscal and external deficits.[1] The resulting forecast is for real GDP growth in OECD countries during the early 1990s that continues at the 1980s annual average of about 2.6 percent. Under this scenario, real interest rates (as represented by the six-month Eurodollar rate) fall back from an average of 5.5 percent in the 1980s to about 3 percent, enabling some revival of growth in Latin America without aggravating the debt-service burden.

The World Bank estimates under this modestly favorable scenario that average annual real GDP growth in Latin America would recover to about 3.1 percent, or 1.2 percent on a per-capita basis, after subtracting population growth. Alternatively, without adjustments to reduce fiscal and trade imbalances and permit some easing in monetary policy, particularly in the United States, Latin American per-capita growth would post virtually no increase.

At this time, the favorable scenario of policy adjustments and continued modest economic growth has been clouded by several uncertainties. The determination to reduce the U.S. fiscal imbalance is eroding with signs of further weakness in the American economy. Tax increases and spending cuts to deal with the deficit have an increased chance of pushing the economy into recession. A further complication is the renewed instability in the Middle East, triggered by the Iraqi invasion of Kuwait. Although it seems unlikely that oil prices will be sustained at sharply higher levels in the range of $28 to $30 per barrel, if indeed these price levels hold, the risks of pushing the U.S. economy into recession are significant. Because of the sheer size of the U.S. economy, a pronounced downturn of -2 percent growth for two quarters or more would damage prospects for a revival in Latin America, since the region still sells exports primarily in the American market.

It should be stressed that even if the previously mentioned complications do not push the industrial world into recession, the favorable scenario of continued growth results in only modest improvement for Latin America relative to other regions of the world. An average annual per-capita income growth of 1 to 2 percent, which seems most likely for the region, will lag that of the affluent OECD by a full percentage point per year and will be less than one-third the per-capita growth projected for Asia. The relatively weaker per-capita growth recovery in Latin America reflects in part the region's higher population growth.

Latin American growth also continues to fall short of that in Asia and the OECD countries, because the region remains relatively more dependent on primary product exports. With the easing of interest rates and the strong requirements to invest in a modern productive capacity, especially in Eastern Europe and Latin America, metal and other material prices should firm up. However, overall primary product prices in real terms will continue to decline slowly in the 1990s. Long-term structural changes in the world economy will result in a declining relative demand for material inputs, as we will discuss in the next section.

Oil prices remain an important determinant of external balance in the oil-exporting countries of Mexico, Venezuela, Ecuador, and Colombia. These countries have begun to diversify their economies and export earnings away from the petroleum sector. The structural change is most dramatic in the case of Mexico, where the share of oil in total export earnings fell from 69 percent in 1984 to an estimated 35 percent in 1990. Nevertheless, large changes in oil prices can still have a significant impact on the ability of these oil-exporting countries to meet their debt payments. Even in the more diversified Mexican economy of today, the petroleum-sector export earnings match interest payments on external debt.

Forecasts of oil prices have been significantly complicated by the renewed instability in the Middle East, following Iraq's invasion of Kuwait. Until these developments, prospects were that world oil prices will increase over time in line with inflation in manufactured goods prices, but with considerable fluctuations. The lesson for OPEC from the sharp price increases in the 1970s was that large increases in oil prices in a short time will trigger demand adjustments that can lead to an oversupply of oil and lower long-term income for oil exporters. But now it is difficult to forecast future collective OPEC behavior because of the tensions between the Gulf region states following the Iraqi invasion. However, given the willingness to keep oil supplies stable by compensating adjustments, by Saudi Arabia and Venezuela initially, and the substantial stocks of oil in private and government reserves, the chances are still reasonable that oil price trends will follow a more orderly path than in the 1970s. But in the longer run, the decline in capacity from non-OPEC suppliers, like the United States and the North Sea, and the emergence of upper-income developing countries, especially in Asia, as energy consumers, will put a slowly rising floor under oil prices.

The renewed conflict in the Middle East has had two specific effects in Latin America. First, Venezuela has taken an early lead in offering to increase oil production to help offset lost production from conflict zones in the Persian gulf. This action reinforces the new spirit of hemispheric cooperation that developed in 1990. Second, Brazil is put in a difficult position in terms of its trade strategy, because it relies extensively on barter trade with Iraq, which has now become an unreliable supplier of oil in this barter exchange.

PROTECTIONIST TRENDS

Given the continued pressure on Latin American governments to open their economies to world competitive influences, the region has a strong claim on the industrial counties to keep the world trading system open. However, while world trade continues to grow at more than double the rate of world output, the international trading system has become less liberal. Seven rounds of multilateral trade negotiations since 1945 have significantly reduced tariff barriers to the industrial countries. But export markets for Latin America have been increasingly constrained by nontariff barriers, such as "safeguard actions," voluntary export restraint arrangements in steel, for example, the multifiber textile agreement, and continued restrictive quotas on imports of lower-cost tropical agricultural products, particularly sugar. The World Bank estimates that about 20 percent of the exports from developing countries are affected by nontariff barriers, which is about twice the impact on exports from industrial countries.[2]

There is also a real danger that Latin America, as well as the United States, will be left out of a growing trade under bilateral, common market, or free-trade arrangements, notably the enlarged European market. The impact on Latin America of the dramatic integration of Europe will be discussed in a later section of this chapter.

The current and eighth round of multilateral trade talks, the Uruguay round, has been extended into 1991. This round of trade talks has been especially difficult because the agenda tackled new and difficult issues, such as freer trade in agriculture, the opening up of markets for services, and intellectual property rights. Latin American countries have felt very much like outsiders at previous multilateral negotiations, but are more actively involved in this Uruguay round. Latin American and other developing countries seek to link access to their markets for service trade to a reduction in barriers to exporting into industrial countries. For example, it is encouraging that the OECD has agreed to phase out the multifiber quantitative restrictions in textiles, although only gradually over fifteen years. Liberalization of trade in agriculture would be particularly beneficial to Argentina and Brazil.

The prospects for improving access to the industrial country markets for Latin American products are being profoundly affected by the discussions to forge a free-trade area between Mexico and the United States. Mexico has moved far more rapidly than any other Latin American country, except Chile, to convert quantitative restrictions on imports to tariffs and then to reduce the average tariff rates. In addition, it is proposed that Mexico would move to free trade with the United States, similar to the agreement that has been negotiated between Canada and the United States.

The Bush administration in mid–1990 has begun an initiative to improve economic and trade relations with Latin America, building on the momentum in trade talks with Mexico and Canada. There is growing mutual interest in freer trade in the Western Hemisphere, given the concern about being discriminated against in the European Common Market.

The final global influence on Latin American economic prospects in the 1990s are trends in exchange rates. Latin American currencies will continue to depreciate relative to the U.S. dollar in line with the higher inflation in the region. In turn, the U.S. dollar is likely to continue to depreciate relative to the European currency bloc and the Japanese yen. This prospect is due to the persistance of the U.S. trade deficit and the relatively less favorable spread of U.S. interest rates, since the U.S. economy is likely to continue growing more slowly than Europe and Asia.

This further depreciation of the dollar relative to other major currencies could be mildly favorable to Latin America. Higher growth rates and pressure to reduce surpluses in Europe and Asia should stimulate exports to non-dollar markets, while a recovery in Latin America, biased toward investment rather than consumption, might favor imports from the United States. We will examine the changing direction in Latin American trade later.

There is no reliable information on the currency denomination of Latin American debt, but recent trends have been for U.S. banks to lose market share in trade finance to European banks. Nevertheless, it is likely that the currency denomination of finance is linked to the currency earned in exports, so that exposure to currency fluctuations in debt servicing is minimal.

In conclusion, the global economic environment is likely to be modestly favorable for a revival of Latin American growth in the 1990s. Industrial countries should avoid a major recession, but the growth leadership will lie with Europe and Asia, historically less important markets for Latin America than the United States. Consistent with the outlook for growth, commodity and oil prices are not likely to experience the sharp increases seen in the 1970s, barring a major collapse of production in the Middle East. Real interest rates should move lower, and the dollar will continue to depreciate against other major currencies. However, in assessing prospects for Latin America, it is important to look beyond the forecast of aggregate output to the changing structure of the world economy. The changing structure and how Latin America fits into that change is the subject of the next section.

CHANGED WORLD ECONOMIC STRUCTURE

It is a well-established observation that in the process of economic development over decades, the composition of output and employment shifts from primary activity (farming, fishing, and mining) to secondary, or manufacturing, and then to tertiary, or service, activity. Peter Drucker in a seminal article in *Foreign Affairs* highlights this change in world economic structure.[3] He discusses two fundamental and permanent changes in the economic structure that have profound and disturbing implications for Latin America in the 1990s. These changes are indeed disturbing for the United States as well, compared to the advanced countries of Europe and Northern Asia (Japan, Korea, Taiwan, Hong Kong, and Singapore).

In global terms, first, the primary-products economy has come "uncoupled" from the industrial economy; and, second, in the industrial economy, production has come "uncoupled" from employment.

First, regarding the primary-products economy, food output is accelerating rapidly as world population growth slows. This is a disturbing trend for Latin American countries, such as Argentina, Brazil, and Colombia, which still rely heavily on agriculture for export earnings. Ten years ago, the Club of Rome and the Carter administration's Global 2000 report warned of world food shortages. Food demand has indeed grown about as fast as expected, but food supply has increased much faster than forecast. Farm output in China and India, which account for 40 percent of the world's population, have outstripped earlier forecasts, leaving those two giant countries nearly self-sufficient in food. Furthermore, there have been dramatic reductions in food-storage losses due to pests and rot, especially in India.

Looking ahead, technological change in irrigation, soil use, and disease control are likely to sustain rapid growth on agricultural yield. As a result, import markets for food have diminished. The major remaining importers are Japan and the Soviet Union, and the economic revolution beginning in the U.S.S.R. may well improve food output there. Thus, in the long run, the best prospects for improved farm exports from Argentina and Brazil, as well as the United States, may well be the phasing out of heavy subsidies to inefficient farming in Europe, which is a subject of intense debate in the Uruguay round trade negotiations.

Turning to nonfarm commodities, world market prospects are also gloomy. A study by the International Monetary Fund in 1985 estimated that the amount of industrial raw materials needed to produce one unit of industrial output is about 40 percent of what was required in 1900.[4] This decline is particularly dramatic in recent manufacturing in Japan. In general, both old and new industries use less raw material. For example, as Drucker points out, 50 to 100 pounds of fiberglass cable can carry as many phone calls as one ton of copper wire, and far less energy is required to produce this cable.[5]

Another reason for declining relative demand for industrial materials is the lower importance of materials in the faster growing, new technology industries.

For example, in semiconductor chips, the backbone of the fast-growing consumer electronics industry, raw materials account for less than 3 percent of total production costs, compared to 40 percent in automobiles.

These trends in world demand for agriculture and raw materials are disturbing, given the export structure of Latin American economies. Although these economies have diversified export earnings away from primary products to manufactures, the diversification has proceeded more rapidly in Asia. World Bank data show that the share of primary products in total exports from Latin America declined from 93 percent in 1965 to 67 percent in 1987. However, in that same time, the share in East Asian exports fell from 75 to 27 percent, and for South Asia, from 63 to 34 percent.

The second fundamental change, cited by Peter Drucker, is the uncoupling of manufacturing output from employment of labor.[6] The absolute as well as the relative decline in factory ("blue collar") employment in the advanced industrial countries is already well established over the last four decades. However, actual manufacturing output has continued to increase. This implies that there has been a continuing process of improved productivity of labor in manufacturing by means of automation, computerized control of production and inventory management, and other innovations. The more dynamic industrialized economies, such as Japan, Germany, and France, accept this change by encouraging factory workers to retrain, rather than trying to hold on to particular factory jobs, as has been more the tendency in the United States and Great Britain.

Drucker's strongly stated conclusion on this trend is that countries as well as companies must "sharply increase manufacturing production and at the same time sharply reduce the blue-collar work force" if they are to "remain competitive—or even to remain 'developed.' "[7]

This process can be described as moving up a "ladder of technology" and is proceeding most dramatically across the spectrum of Asian countries at different stages of development. Japan has systematically planned to move its older, labor-intensive industries—first textiles, later cars, now even simple computer production offshore to lower labor cost countries in Asia. The relocation was first directed, ten to twenty years ago, to the four East Asian economies with sufficient infrastructure and labor discipline to absorb relatively sophisticated production processes—Korea, Taiwan, Hong Kong, and Singapore. These countries, in turn, are now relatively high labor-cost environments for the older, low-technology industries such as textiles and shoes, which have been further relocated to lower-wage countries such as China, Thailand, and Indonesia.

This dynamic process of development is a dual one of aging technologies cascading down the ladder from more advanced to less advanced countries, whereas countries that have successfully invested in infrastructure, new manufacturing capacity, and education move up the ladder to higher levels of technology. For countries at the top of the technology ladder, like Japan, the emphasis is increasingly on knowledge or information-based industries, such as information processing, telecommunications, and pharmaceuticals. In the most advanced countries, these industries are now the leading growth sectors, rather than industries that process raw materials into more finished form, but still contain relatively little knowledge input, like clothing, fabricated metal products, and even motor vehicles.

However, a significant number of material-based industries continue to operate in the most advanced, high labor-cost countries, due to remarkable advances in automation and the use of robots on the shop floor. This replacement of human workers by machines has given a renewed life for industries, such as textiles and television production, in high-wage countries that had suffered labor-intensive foreign competition.

The implications of this process of technology and economic development for Latin America in the 1990s are disturbing, because the trend is to downgrade labor costs as an important competitive factor. But after a decade of austerity, all that many Latin American countries can offer as a production advantage is indeed low-cost labor. For a developing country to move up the ladder of technology just described, there needs to be a commitment not only to continuing investment in physical infrastructure and new manufacturing capacity, but, looking ahead, increasingly to improved education and knowledge.

Governments in Latin America, as elsewhere, should play an active role in promoting both investment in physical infrastructure and human infrastructure— that is, increasing levels of education to cope with modern technology. However, the prescription of fiscal austerity, which is correct in dealing with the persistent problem of inflation and macroeconomic instability, has severely constrained the ability of Latin American countries to sustain these vital investments, essential to moving up the technology ladder. There is a clear tendency to sacrifice investment in physical infrastructure, such as roads, telecommunications, and power distribution, because they have foreign-exchange costs and are politically less sensitive than cuts in government payrolls and current spending.

There is evidence that education that emphasizes math and science training, so essential if labor is to work with newer technologies, falls short in Latin America, not only compared to Europe, the United States, and Japan, but also compared to other Asian countries (whose per-capita income levels are comparable to those in Latin America). Although Latin American objectives for education in high-technology skills are still understandably limited compared to industrialized countries, the more advanced Latin American countries send fewer students for technical education in the United States compared to some developing countries in Asia.

Underinvestment in new human and physical infrastructure is a worry that the United States shares with Latin America. Particularly compared to Japan, American physical facilities are aging faster and our educational achievement level in math and science falls far short of that in Japan.

Table 8.1
Latin America's Direction of Trade (U.S. $ millions)

Latin America	1981 Exports to	1981 Imports from	1989 Exports to	1989 Imports from
United States	37,882 (34.2%)	39,652 (32.7%)	43,011 (35.9%)	39,494 (36.2%)
Eur. Community	23,291 (21.0%)	21,458 (17.7%)	28,365 (23.7%)	21,168 (20.4%)
Japan	5,000 (4.5%)	7,655 (6.3%)	7,164 (5.9%)	6,460 (6.2%)
Asia (ex. Japan)	3,274 (3.0%)	4,140 (3.4%)	7,624 (6.3%)	3,551 (3.4%)
Latin America	23,101 (20.9%)	23,643 (19.5%)	16,533 (13.8%)	17,970 (17.4%)
Canada	3,393 (3.1%)	2,835 (2.3%)	2,639 (2.2%)	2,160 (2.1%)
Other	14,818 (13.3%)	22,004 (18.1%)	14,579 (12.2%)	12,746 (12.3%)
World	110,759 (100%)	121,387 (100%)	119,915 (100%)	103,549 (100%)

Source: International Monetary Fund, *Directory of Trade Statistics, 1986–1989* (Washington,
   D.C.: International Monetary Fund, 1940), and data for Taiwan.
( ) = percent share of the world.

LATIN AMERICA'S INTERNATIONAL ECONOMIC RELATIONS

To understand more fully Latin America's options in the world economy in the
1990s, we need to assess the region's current international economic relations.
The most concrete measure is the composition of regional trade. Table 8.1 shows
Latin America's exports and imports to major markets for 1981 and 1989, derived
from the International Monetary Fund, *Directory of Trade Statistics*. The data
show that Latin America's exports and imports remain heavily concentrated with
the United States, followed by the European Community. Trade with Japan and
Asia is much smaller, but has increased as a percentage of total trade from 1981
to 1989.

   The increase from 1981 to 1989 in the share of Latin American exports going
to the United States and, at a much lower volume level, to Japan and Asia was
largely at the expense of intraregional exports. This reflects the depressed regional
economy and the need to improve hard-currency earnings to service external
debt. On the import side, imports in 1989 were still absolutely lower than 1981

levels. Declining percentage shares indicate that the fall in imports was most pronounced for intraregional trade, for reasons already mentioned on the export side, and from "other" countries, primarily oil imports. World oil prices fell sharply in 1986, and energy demand declined in the depressed Latin economies.

Of course, trade flows are only one aspect of international economic relations, which also include capital movements and trade in services. Data on service and investment flows are difficult to obtain by country of origin. Relations with government and commercial creditors are discussed in Chapters 2 and 5, respectively, of this book. Nevertheless, the direction of trade flows is a good starting point for discussing prospects for external support for Latin American recovery in the 1990s.

THE CONTRASTING CAPACITY OF THE UNITED STATES AND JAPAN

Although the trade relationship with the United States is dominant, it is unlikely to be leveraged by a substantial increase in official or commercial finance from the United States. The U.S. federal government budget restraint, especially in view of the mounting costs of the savings-and-loan bailout, remains a very real deterrent to a meaningful increase in official aid or credits to any world region, except the Middle East, where Iraqi expansion threatens America's strategic interest in oil supplies.

On the commercial side, U.S. banks are preoccupied with their domestic survival and are giving a low strategic priority to even well-defined trade and project credits to Latin America, following painful writeoffs of sovereign Latin American debt. Recent indications are that significant increases in trade between U.S. companies and Latin American customers are being financed to a far greater extent by non-U.S., particularly European, banks, which do not face such pressing problems of consolidation and capital adequacy, as do U.S. banks.

U.S. companies are more likely to step up business with the region, as Latin America shows signs of renewed economic stability. However, American firms will be constrained by limited credit and guarantees from Washington and U.S. banks and will turn increasingly to European and Japanese financing.

In mid–1990, President Bush announced a new trade and finance initiative toward Latin America called the "Enterprise for the Americas." Following on earlier discussions about a free-trade zone between Mexico and the United States, the new initiative aims for a hemisphericwide trade zone. The proposal was enhanced with modest new money for privatization and environmental preservation. The initiative also significantly offered to write down Latin debts owed to the U.S. government. However, the initiative is necessarily long on aspirations and short on funding, and was subsequently upstaged by the crisis in the Middle East.

There is currently a much greater capacity in Japan, possibly also Taiwan and

Korea, and in Europe to finance a recovery in Latin America, but is it in their strategic interest?

Turning first to Japan and Asia, Table 8.1 shows only a modest, though rising, share in trade with Latin America by Japan and other Asian countries. However, the trade data understate the financial capacity and potential interest that the Pacific region could play in a larger commercial role with Latin America in the 1990s. This interest is developing from both sides of the Latin American–Asia economic relationship.

On the Latin American side, the region's orientation was historically and culturally toward Europe, and economically and strategically to the United States. Asia was a remote and exotic region of little interest. Latin American policy makers rationalized their external debt problem as just part of a general "Third World" debt problem, without realizing (or acknowledging) that developing debtor countries in Asia, notably Korea, had adjusted to and overcome the debt problem far more successfully. Only in the last years of the 1980s did Latin America, led by Chile, begin to look toward Asia as a successful and possibly relevant model of development, in contrast to the continuing crisis in their own region.

Latin Americans also became aware of the rising economic and financial power of Japan and saw the growing role that Japan was playing in the succeeding rounds of debt restructuring in Latin America. Fascination (and fear) of Japanese business prowess and culture developed earlier in the United States, because of the much larger and more open trade and investment relationship with Japan. But in the latter part of the 1980s, Latin American leaders began to travel to Tokyo, as well as to other Asian capitals, if only because it was evident that Japan was displacing the United States as the "rich uncle" in international finance.

It has been American leaders, like Secretary Baker in a June 1989 speech to the Asian Society, who evoked the picture of the nations of the Pacific Rim. Indeed, the Pacific washes the shores of two Latin American nations that have shown the most active interest in Asia—Chile and Mexico. Peru has a new president of Japanese descent, Alberto Fujimoro, who has turned early in his administration to Tokyo for assistance with Peru's enormous economic problems. Brazil is another country with an active interest in Asia because of its huge natural resource attraction for Asian industry and its large Japanese population, the largest outside of Japan.

Although Brazil remains an attractive prospect for Asian investment because of its diverse and large natural resources and huge internal market, Mexico offers the more significant near-term opportunities due to the success of the Salinas government in stabilizing the economy and reducing import restrictions. In a particularly interesting symbol of a significant reorientation of Mexican policy toward Japan, President Salinas sends his children to a Japanese school in Mexico city and on summer vacations to Japan.

Although there are clear signs of increased Latin American interest in Asia, the more important question is whether Asia, which holds the purse strings, is really interested in investing in Latin America. From the perspective of the ladder of technology (discussed earlier), the low-wage, resource-rich countries of South Asia are likely to continue getting much more attention from the cash-rich advanced countries of North Asia than will Latin America. However, there are two reasons why Latin America can hope to see substantially expanded economic relations with Asia in the 1990s: first, the sheer size of the financial surplus that Japan, the world's largest creditor, has to deploy around the world, and, second, the sourcing base that Latin American countries can offer for sales into the increasingly protectionist U.S. market.

Japan has displaced the United States as the world's largest creditor nation, with net foreign assets approaching $400 billion. The top ten banks in the world are Japanese, and Japanese companies are now found ranked in the top ten world companies across many industries.

Although Japan has recently played a more active role in restructuring Latin American debt, particularly in Mexico, it is estimated that Japanese banks hold only $30 billion of Latin American debt, totaling about $300 billion, or about 40 percent of debt held by U.S. banks. According to the Morgan Bank, cumulative foreign direct investment by Japan in Latin America in 1988 is about $9 billion, if investments in offshore financial centers and ships with Panamanian registration are excluded. This adjusted level is far below cumulative investment in the United States ($72 billion), Europe ($30 billion), and Asia ($32 billion).[8]

While Japan will continue to dominate in investment from Asia, Taiwan, with $70 billion of foreign-exchange reserves, has begun to invest more in both the United States and Latin America. There is also some activity by Korean firms.

Latin America offers a strategic location for supplying the U.S. markets with products from Asian companies. Direct sales from Asia to the United States have been increasingly constrained by protectionist sentiments. Furthermore, the elimination by the U.S. government of preferential tariff treatment for Hong Kong, Taiwan, Korea, and Singapore impels both Japan and these other Asian countries to relocate manufacturing for the U.S. market in Latin American countries, which are likely to continue enjoying preferential access to the American market.

The most concrete manifestation of this relocation of production is the operation of Japanese firms in Mexican assembly plants, or "maquila," which pay no U.S. tariff on the Mexican value added for products sold in the United States. Although American firms still lead in the use of Mexican maquila plants, the U.S. government estimates that there will be 1,000 Japanese facilities by 1995. There have been some Korean investments in the assembly plants in Mexico as well.

Japanese businesses with their well-known capacity for taking the long strategic view will position themselves in Mexico to take advantage of a possible evolution toward a United States–Mexico free-trade zone, which began to be discussed more seriously in 1990.

In a recent article, Guttman and Laughlin catalogue a variety of Asian investment initiatives in Latin America that is interesting but not yet substantial in dollar amount.[9] Japan is investing in new or expanded automobile production in Brazil and Mexico and is taking an active role in the development of production and refining by Pemex, Mexico's oil company. In Chile, Japan has become the leading consumer of forestry products and has participated in the investment consortium for La Escondida, the world's largest copper project. Japan is also making investments that could make Chile into the world's leading iodine producer by 1995. Korea is talking with Peru about a barter agreement to exchange cars and electronic technology for coal. Taiwan is developing an export-processing zone in Costa Rica.[10]

In conclusion, although Asian prospects in Latin America are not likely to be as attractive an investment location as Southeast Asia already is, the sheer size of financial surpluses in Japan and Taiwan and the prefered access to the U.S. market from a Latin American location suggest significant trade and investment growth from Asia in the 1990s.

Can the same be said for Europe?

ECONOMIC RELATIONS BETWEEN EUROPE AND LATIN AMERICA

Latin America has long looked to Europe for its historical and cultural roots, seeking to offset the weighty influence of the United States in the Western Hemisphere. Liberal and socialist groups in European countries took an active interest in the democratic movement in Latin America, and often stood with Latin American intellectual leaders against U.S. policy in the region, particularly Central America.

Ideological interest in the development of democracy does not translate into an important economic relationship between Europe and Latin America. Table 8.1 shows that Europe was the destination of 24 percent of Latin American exports in 1989 and the source of 20 percent of the region's imports. Considering that the European Community includes three of the five largest economies in the non-Communist world (Germany, France, and Italy), these trading volumes are not particularly large.

In theory, the complementarity between the economies of Europe and Latin America should promote trade. Latin America is a potential source of labor-intensive manufactured products, tropical foodstuffs, minerals, and forestry products, as well as some temperate-zone farm products from Argentina. However, protectionist policies in Europe have restricted the growth of imports of manufactures and farm products that compete directly with higher-cost producers in Europe. Former colonies of Europe in Africa and Asia supply tropical products and minerals that Latin America can also provide. Imports by Latin America of capital goods and more sophisticated consumer goods from Europe have been limited by the foreign-exchange shortage in Latin America and competition from the older and larger presence of U.S. business.

Prospects for aid and investment are not particularly promising either. Although European countries have commited a higher percentage of their national income to foreign assistance than either the United States or Japan, the aid is targeted to the lowest-income countries in Asia and Africa, and Bolivia and Haiti in the Western Hemisphere. Despite a decade of economic decline, income levels in Latin America remain too high to qualify for foreign aid.

There were some substantial European business investments in Latin America, particularly by German and Swedish firms in Brazil. However, as with U.S. direct investment, new initiatives will wait for evidence of greater macroeconomic stability in Argentina and Brazil and a more favorable regulatory environment in Mexico.

European banks are in a much better position than U.S. banks to take on new lending to Latin America, having written off most sovereign loans and set up sizeable reserves. However, because the region is a relatively low priority for the domestic corporate customers of European banks and Latin debt poses no problem for bank balance sheets, European banks tend to take a tough line on new lending. This was evident in the unwillingness of European banks to put new money into Mexico under the Brady Plan. As already mentioned, however, there is some indication that European banks are willing to step up short-term trade finance, even between U.S. companies and Latin America, particularly Mexico, because the risk–reward trade-offs for this business are attractive.

The more complete integration of the twelve members of the European Community by 1992 and the rapid opening up of Eastern Europe to Western European business will result in an even lower priority for trade, investment, and foreign assistance for Latin America. First of all, there will be a strong tendency of the higher-income European countries to divert imports of labor-intensive manufactures from Latin America to suppliers in the lower-wage countries of Southern Europe, such as Portugal, Spain, and Greece, as all internal customs barriers come down. Second, there are now tremendous competing claims from Eastern Europe for financial assistance to ease the transition from centralized socialistic to private economies. Third, although it will be difficult to launch competitive enterprises in Eastern Europe, such firms using lower-cost but educated labor could be a significant competitive threat to not only Latin American, but also, manufacturers in Southern Europe.

Within Europe, it is Germany and Spain that are most likely to pursue economic relations with Latin America for political and cultural reasons. Howard Wiarda in a recent article points out that "each of Germany's major political parties has its own foundation, or 'stiftung,' which operates in Latin America to further the interests of both the party and the nation."[11] Wiarda suggests that the newly emerging democratic institutions in Latin America have common ties with German groups and this leads to greater interest in economic ties.

Spain is the most obvious link for Latin America into the European Community. The dynamic socialist government of Felipé Gonzalez in the democratic post-Franco Spain has been a very attractive model for Spanish-speaking Latin

American countries as they struggle with the return to democracy. As Wiarda points out, Spain had for a time considered conditioning its entry into the European Community to the maintenance of trade preferences with Latin America, somewhat like the Lome convention arrangements with former European colonies in Africa.[12] However, Spain is now preoccupied with its competitive survival in the European market after 1992, and with the opening up of Eastern Europe, which threatens to divert both financial aid and investment from Spain to the East. These pressing development and business interests suggest that even Spain will give low priority to finding a trading niche for Latin America in the European Community.

Latin American trade and financial relations with Eastern Europe will be profoundly affected by the dramatic opening up of the Soviet political and economic system, the radical reforms in Eastern Europe, and the effective end of the Cold War era. There has been some barter or special bilateral trade of the U.S.S.R. and Eastern European countries with some countries in Latin America, notably Argentina and Brazil, in farm products, oil, and machinery. With the disruption of production and the emphasis on hard-currency trade in Eastern Europe, the existing Latin American trade will be renewed only to the extent that it is competitive by international standards.

The end of the Cold War and the severe budget problems faced by the U.S.S.R. will cause Moscow to take a very hard look at its costly subsidy of the Cuban economy, amounting to over $3 billion per year. The collapse of the Castro regime in Cuba is now a real possibility. The result could be a flourishing of the Cuban economy, nourished by the talents and considerable finances of Cuban emigres from the United States. This would be a significant expansionary influence in the Caribbean and Central America.

In conclusion, during the 1990s, European countries with a previously active interest in Latin America, particularly Germany and Spain, will be greatly preoccupied with adjusting to the competitive influences of the enlarged European market after 1992. This strategic challenge has been significantly complicated by the surprisingly rapid opening up of the economies in Eastern Europe. It will be difficult for Latin American economies to expand trade with Europe because of the competition from Southern Europe inside a market free of barriers and from emerging low-wage markets in Eastern Europe. The potential opening of Cuba to a private economy will be a positive factor for Latin America.

CONCLUSION

As mentioned at the beginning of this chapter, the recovery of Latin America in the 1990s will depend primarily on its own domestic economic policies. These include first and foremost macroeconomic stabilization, followed by a significant restructuring of the economies to encourage private-sector investment. The growth of Latin America will be more sensitive to favorable world economic conditions, if the open-economy policies of Chile and, more recently, Mexico become the norm for the region.

The global economic environment should be generally favorable, with sustained growth led by Europe and Asia and lower interest rates. However, there could be severe disruptions in the form of stagflation, via the world oil market, if the current instability in the Middle East is not controlled. Furthermore, the structure of future world growth, with its emphasis on knowledge-intensive industries and a reduced role for material and labor-intensive production puts Latin American economies at a disadvantage, particularly compared to Asian economies.

It is reasonable to conclude that Latin America will be left outside of emerging trading blocs in Europe and Asia. This is a risk that also faces the United States. In Europe, government and business strategy is preoccupied with achieving a smooth integration between high- and low-wage regions in Western Europe and also with newly emerging private sectors in Eastern Europe. In this environment, there is little incentive to accommodate Latin American trade and investment requirements.

Nevertheless, it would be a mistake for Latin America to revert to an import-substitution strategy, closing the region to international competitive influences, as long as the U.S. economy remains open to trade with the region. The proposed United States—Mexico free-trade zone and initiatives by the Bush administration in mid–1990 indicate that the United States remains committed to open trade with Latin America.

Japan, and to a lesser extent, Taiwan and Korea have the capacity and interest in expanding trade and investment in Latin America, since it is a region of preferred access to the United States, a market that they can no longer easily source from Asia. Latin American leaders are increasingly aware of the benefits of a closer relationship with Asia. However, they need to signal a new attitude of welcome to prospective Asian, as well as U.S. and European, investors by means of a pragmatic macroeconomic policy and favorable regulatory conditions for foreign investment.

NOTES

1. The World Bank, *World Development Report, 1989* (Washington, D.C.: The World Bank, 1988).

2. Ibid., p. 2.

3. Peter Drucker, "The Changed World Economy," *Foreign Affairs* (Spring 1986), pp. 766–791.

4. Ibid., p. 773.

5. Ibid.

6. Ibid., p. 776.

7. Ibid., p. 777.

8. Morgan Guaranty Trust Company, "Japan: the World's Leading Foreign Investor," *World Financial Markets* (November 1989), p. 4.

9. William L. Guttman and Scott D. Laughlin, "Latin America in the Pacific Era," *Washington Quarterly* (Spring 1990), pp. 168–181.

10. Ibid.

11. Howard J. Wiarda, "Europe's Ambiguous Relations with Latin America: Blowing Hot and Cold in the Western Hemisphere," *Washington Quarterly* (Spring 1990), pp. 153–167.

12. Ibid., p. 161.

9   A Comparative View of Latin America and South Korea, Turkey, and Morocco

Scott B. MacDonald*

INTRODUCTION

The global debt crisis is usually considered a Latin American affair. Indeed, the largest debtors—Brazil and Mexico—are located in Latin America and are supported by a cast of other heavily indebted countries like Argentina, Peru, and Venezuela.[1] Yet, the debt problem that has dominated the agendas of finance ministers and overshadowed economic programs in the developing world is much more than a Latin American affair. Other countries, such as the Philippines, Jordan, and Nigeria struggled with the debt problem in the 1980s and some are likely to continue to do so in the 1990s.

This chapter examines the other side of the debt crisis, where there has been relative success in managing indebtedness and making headway in overall economic development. It is often overlooked that there are countries beyond the Latin American context that have successfully adopted the difficult programs of stabilization and structural adjustment and that some countries never rescheduled in the 1980s. Furthermore, although much of Latin America remains beyond the pale of commercial creditors, other nations in Asia and the Middle East have entered or are in the process of entering a postdebt crisis world that includes a return to international capital markets. Three countries fit that description—South Korea, Turkey, and Morocco. The three are at varying stages of development, with South Korea operating in a postdebt crisis environment. Turkey has almost

*Scott B. MacDonald is an official of the Office of the Comptroller of the Currency (OCC). The views expressed here, however, do not in any fashion represent those of the OCC.

reached that stage, although a number of problems linger, the most recent of which is the impact of the 1990–1991 Persian Gulf crisis. Morocco is still in the process of making fundamental changes, but the direction has been charted and substantial backsliding will be difficult. The three share a common thread of extensive structural adjustment toward an open economy as the correct path to advance the nation into the next century.

The author is aware of the extensive structural adjustment program in Mexico since the de la Madrid administration took office in the mid–1980s. Additionally, the author concedes that other Latin American countries, such as Chile, Costa Rica, Uruguay, and Venezuela, have embarked upon the same path. However, most studies on economic development in the 1980s confirm that it was a "lost decade" for Latin America by practically all economic indicators. As U.S. economist John Williamson noted: "As the decade ended, the region [Latin America] remained mired in stagflation, burdened by foreign debt, disfigured by the world's most inegalitarian income distribution, and crippled by a continuing lack of confidence on the part of not only its foreign creditors but also its own entrepreneurs, manifested in low domestic investment and massive holdings of capital flight."[2] Although South Korea, Turkey, and Morocco had problems, the 1980s were not a lost decade and, in fact, important progress was made in a number of areas.

SOUTH KOREA AS A LITTLE DRAGON

It is important to place South Korea in the proper developmental context as a Little Dragon (also referred to as a Little Tiger or Newly Industrializing Economy, NIE) along with Hong Kong, Singapore, and Taiwan. The Little Dragons represent a small group of nations that share high levels of economic growth and low levels of inflation, place an emphasis on exports, and are capable of rapid market and product diversification.[3] They have also developed dynamic local capital markets. Singapore and Hong Kong, in particular, are regarded as significant international stock markets and offshore financial centers.

When added together, the Little Dragons have a population of roughly 75 million and, in the mid–1980s, had a combined gross national product of around $200 billion, with a growth rate of about 10 percent annually.[4] Together with Japan, they have emerged as part of a dynamic core of the rapidly expanding Pacific Basin economy.[5]

In the 1980s, the Little Dragons outdistanced many of their competitors and increasingly have challenged the European Community, Japan, and the United States for global market share. In the early 1990s, they also represent the other side of the debt crisis: virtually all of the Little Dragons had structural adjustment problems on the road to reaching export-led growth and overall economic stability.

What turned these four developing countries into today's NIEs was the economic and political predicaments that they faced in the 1950s. With low foreign-exchange reserves, dependent in part on U.S. assistance, and confronted with substantial national security concerns, the Little Tigers were forced to downgrade all other aims, no matter how urgent or imperative, and give economic activities top priority.[6] This meant that economic development was a priority over political development, which helps explain the relatively nondemocratic path these countries evolved upon.

In a very broad sense, the key elements of the Little Dragons' rapid emergence on the global economic scene were extensive central control and strong leaders; societies that were usually built on consensus; a desire to raise national consciousness in the face of present or past humilations from Western powers or Imperial Japan; a bureaucratic commitment to the economic priority; a staffing of national bureaucracies with technocrats; a nurturing of the private sector and protection of private ownership of property, especially the means of production; an emphasis on education; and, above all, developing an export-oriented expansion that was flexible and capable of technological leapfrogging when market conditions changed. The fundamental reason the export model took hold in the 1950s and 1960s is summarized by Jon Woronoff " . . . the East Asians sell their exports in order to obtain raw materials, foodstuffs, and capital goods without which they could not continue producing or, to be perfectly frank, simply survive."[7]

The degree of state involvement in each of the Little Dragons has varied. In Taiwan and South Korea, the state has played a role as the most active economic actor, owning property and, to some degree, seeking to shape the conditions in the marketplace. In South Korea, the state was active in encouraging the *chaebol*, a group of unique conglomerates that were initially backed by substantial injections of government credit. In 1988, it was estimated that the chaebols accounted for more than 40 percent of South Korea's GNP.[8]

At the other extreme, Hong Kong is, without doubt, a bastion of laissez-faire trade and capitalism. Singapore has pursued a "liberal" economic path with free-trade policies that were in the late 1980s and early 1990s supplemented by free capital mobility. Despite some differences in their approach to development, the four Little Dragons weathered the debt crisis without rescheduling or severe economic hardships. Although there were concerns about South Korea, which had borrowed heavily, the Asian NIEs did not go through a lost decade as in the Latin American case. Table 9.1 reflects some of the key differences between the Little Dragons and the major Latin American debtors.

South Korea, in many respects, represents one of the most dramatic turnarounds in terms of the global debt crisis. Although each of the Little Dragons has an impressive story of economic expansion based on the export-growth model, South Korea was the only NIE that used extensive external borrowing to accelerate its development and to cope with external shocks (like the 1973–1974 oil-price hikes). Moreover, it underwent a process of democratization in the 1980s, drawing a point of comparison with many of the Latin American debtors.

Table 9.1
Rate of Real Gross Domestic Product (GDP) Growth and Rate of GDP Per-Capita Growth (%)

	1963–73 GDP	1963–73 GDP per capita	1973–85 GDP	1973–85 GDP per capita
Hong Kong	8.2	6.0	8.7	6.3
Korea	9.6	7.1	7.3	5.7
Singapore	11.6	9.5	7.9	6.5
Taiwan	10.7	7.6	7.9	5.9
Argentina	4.8	3.2	0.2	-1.4
Brazil	8.3	5.5	4.3	1.9
Mexico	7.8	4.4	4.8	1.9

Source: Bela Balssa and John Williamson, *Adjusting to Success: Balance of Payments Policy in the East Asian NIEs* (Washington, D.C.: Institute for International Economics, 1987), pp. 2–3.

South Korea's early years were dominated by tremendous political turmoil with first the division of the Korean Peninsula in 1945 and then the Korean War (1950–1953). The post-Korean War governments were largely concerned with political survival, and economic matters were secondary. Threats to political survival, it should be pointed out, came from both within the country in the form of rival military factions, student riots, or the political parties and from across the northern frontier, where the Kim Il-Sung regime maintained a large army, ready to march south to reunite the peninsula under communist rule. However, during the long rule of General Park Chung Hee, who came to power by a coup in 1961, the economy received primary attention. In October 1979, Park was assassinated, but the legacy he left behind was one of the developing world's major economic success stories.

Park's death put the Korean development model of export-led growth and heavy borrowing to develop industrial infrastructure and greater export capacity through a severe testing period. Although the economy grew by 7.4 percent in 1979, it contracted by 3 percent in 1980 and there was speculation that Korea would not be able to regain its momentum. Further concerns were raised as the world recession deepened in the early 1980s and interest rates rose. Moreover, after 1982, the global debt crisis brought Korea under renewed scrutiny: the East Asian country's external debt had grown from $7.4 billion in 1975 to $29.5 billion in 1980.[9] By 1982, its external debt reached $37.3 billion, equal to 52.3

Table 9.2
Selected Economic Indicators for South Korea
(in U.S. $ billions)

	1982	1985	1986	1987	1988
Exports*	28.4	33.1	42.0	56.3	70.9
Imports*	31.5	34.6	38.4	47.6	58.1
International					
Reserves	2.95	2.97	3.4	3.7	12.5
Current Account					
Bal. of Payments	−2.65	−.887	4.6	9.85	14.2
Total Ext. Debt	37.3	47.2	46.7	40.5	37.2

Source: The World Bank, *World Debt Tables, 1989–90, Vol. 2* (Washington, D.C.: The World Bank), p. 202.
*Exports or imports of goods and services.

percent of GNP. Although the debt-service ratio was 19.7 percent, GDP growth slowed from 1981's 7.4 percent to 1982's 5.7 percent. As international credit markets tightened, it was noted that Korea was the largest debtor in Asia, and about fourth in the developing world behind Brazil, Mexico, and Argentina.

Despite the concern that South Korea would join the ranks of rescheduling countries, it managed to maintain a strong forward momentum in the 1980s. In the 1986–1990 period, South Korea's performance can only be described as impressive. The country's chaebol, having benefitted from government largesse, especially during the Park years, spearheaded Korea's penetration of the U.S. and Canadian auto industries, captured 10 percent of the world memory-chip business, and launched nearly as many ships as Japan. Once perceived as a potential candidate for Latin-style debt problems, this Little Dragon reduced its total external debt, built up its international reserves, posted economic growth of over 10 percent annually (until 1989's estimated 6.5 percent), and controlled inflation well under 10 percent. Table 9.2 demonstrates South Korea's improvements.

Estimates for 1989 indicate that although the pace of economic growth slowed to 6.5 percent, total external debt was further reduced to $30.5 billion (as of September 1989).[10] Moreover, foreign assets (mainly international reserves) expanded by $3.5 billion from January to September 1989 to total $27.4 billion, putting South Korea at the edge of becoming a net creditor.

South Korea's economic success has also come at a time of political uncertainties. In the 1985–1988 period, considerable opposition arose to the ongoing nature of military-dominated authoritarian governments. The opposition widened and exerted pressure on the government to undertake a political liberalization. The ultimate results were relatively fair elections and a more open political system in which the opposition through its representation at the National Assembly has a voice. In 1990, political reform took another step forward when the government party entered into discussions with the two leading opposition parties to create a larger party based on the Liberal Democratic Party (LDP) in Japan. Further, despite certain frictions between the country's regions, there appears to be an evolution of a consensus within the leadership elite (especially if a party merger occurs) that bodes well for further political development, not political turmoil.

In the 1990s, South Korea's major concerns will not be external debt management, but such issues as further trade and financial markets liberalization, a gradual withdrawal of the state from the commanding heights of the economy and the need to maintain open relations with key trading partners, like the United States and Japan as well as the European Community. There will also be an effort to restructure the economy toward a more technologically sophisticated industrial base, while developing a deeper domestic market. The ongoing nature of the political experiment with democracy and the improvement in the standard of living also command attention. South Korea, like the other Little Dragons, will continue to look forward.

THE CASE OF TURKEY

Turkey is not a NIE, but is categorized by the World Bank as a Middle Income Economy, roughly at the same level of development as Chile and Colombia. It has a population of 54 million and has a long and distinct tradition of independence. Unlike the Little Dragons and Latin America, Turkey was never a colony and, in fact, in the form of the Ottoman Empire held sway throughout the Middle East and most of North Africa for a number of centuries. In the First World War, the Ottoman Empire was defeated and dismembered. It was only after a civil war that the Republic was founded in 1923 and foreign occupation of parts of the county ended.

Modern Turkey's problems with external debt management, which resulted in an agreement with commercial banks as early as August 1979, did not occur overnight. The Turkish economy has traditionally been state-driven with public enterprises (State Economic Enterprises, or SEEs) playing a dominant role. Development policies favored import substitution over exports and industry over agriculture. This orientation had its roots in the founding of the Republic in 1923, when the very existence of the country was jeopardized by a number of foreign and internal threats. Although this helped maintain Turkish independence, another result was that, by the 1940s, the government was the nation's major industrial producer, largest employer, and leading exporter.

By the early 1970s, the state-driven Turkish economy was characterized by rapid expansion stimulated by strong industrial growth. This was reflected in 1972 and 1973 by the country's first current account surpluses in over two decades. However, problems emerged: import substitution and heavy industrial-ization required a high level of capital investment because of the need for so-phisticated technology and large-scale production. This resulted in high-cost manufacturing in what was a limited domestic market.

Although the Turkish economy surmounted the oil shock in 1973–1974 by tapping international capital markets, it was unable to halt a widening in the current account deficit. Additionally, as much of its borrowing was short-term, Turkey soon faced a buildup in short-term debt. The situation was further com-plicated by a political crisis in which the two major parties in Parliament rotated in and out of office in a bewildering set of coalitions in the 1977–1979 period. By the second oil-price hike in 1979–1980 and the increase in interest rates at the end of the 1970s, Turkey was in considerable difficulty. The situation was further compounded by the drying up of commercial credits.

Although negotiations with commercial banks were held as early as 1978, the country's political instability precluded any meaningful agreement until after the September 1980 coup. And even then, the country was far from being returned to economic health. The new government, under the guidance of Turgut Ozal, first as Finance Minister and after 1983 as Prime Minister, implemented a sweep-ing structural adjustment program that placed an emphasis on opening up the economy. Along these lines, the new economic policy advanced the liberalization of the trade regime, made use of a flexible exchange-rate policy and a number of minidevaluations, and opened new directions in fiscal and financial services oriented at enhancing the export sector.

The results of the change in direction were significant, especially considering Turkey's historical bent for a restrictive trade regime. The economy expanded at an average rate of 6 percent during the 1984–1986 period, while inflation declined from 50 percent in 1984 to below 30 percent in 1986.[11] There was also a steady improvement in the external accounts. In 1980, total exports were $2.9 billion; by 1984, they had expanded vigorously to $7.4 billion and up to $10.3 billion in 1987.

Although the rate of economic growth slowed in 1988 to 3.5 percent and further to 1.8 percent in 1989 (in part due to drought and a tightening of money supply to cool inflation), the country registered its first current-account surpluses since 1973 and 1974. In 1988, the current-account surplus was $1.5 billion and in 1989 it was $700 million. Although export growth has played an important role in the improvements in the external accounts, the emergence of the tourist sector as a chief foreign-exchange earner ($1 billion in 1989) reflects the wider range of economic restructuring.

The export-growth market has meant diversification of goods exported as well as markets. The composition of exports has continued to shift from agricultural goods to manufactured products, and although the U.S. and European markets are significant, the Middle East and North Africa have emerged in the 1980s as important areas for Turkish commerce. The particular growth areas in industry have been leather goods, textiles, and machinery.

One of the important differences between Turkey and many Latin American debtors is that it was able to return to international capital markets after an absence of several years. While capital for most developing countries dried up after 1982, Turkey cautiously reentered the market in 1983 when it obtained Euro-credits. Although the country's total external debt rose from $19.7 billion in 1982 to $39.6 billion in 1988, according to the World Bank, that capital was needed and well used in the structural adjustment process. Turkey's total external debt, according to the Central Bank, actually fell to $35.3 billion in 1989. This downward trend was helped by the current-account surplus and some currency depreciation.

Renewed capital flows allowed the government to implement its reforms of trade liberalization, the development of nontraditional exports, regional development (as in the southeast) and infrastructural improvements. While many capital-deprived developing countries were forced to neglect and devour their own infrastructures, Turkey was actively improving its, which in part explains how the first of the major debtors to reschedule was one of the first to emerge from the debt crisis. Turkey's September 1989 repayments of the last amounts of rescheduled debt, in this light, were highly symbolic.

Although Turkey has used its new credits for development, debt accumulation has a downside. There can be no hiding the fact that Turkey still has a large external debt. Concerns still exist about the country's ability to pay an annual debt service of around $7 billion (average annual interest and amortization payments in 1987–1991). Unlike South Korea in the 1980s, which was able to grow out of its external debt through trade and current-account surpluses, Turkey's growth has not led to deep net debt reduction. This will remain an objective in the 1990s.

THE CASE OF MOROCCO

While Turkey provides an in-depth examination of the structural adjustment process, Morocco also provides certain insights to the wider dimensions of economic reform. This North African country slid into the debt crisis in the early 1980s. Like Turkey, Morocco's economy was dominated by the state (especially after the Moroccanization program in the early 1970s), which ran most significant enterprises and was largely inward-looking, favoring import substitution. The economy was also highly dependent on the export of phosphates, an important ingredient in fertilizer around the world.

In the 1970s, phosphate prices rose substantially. The Moroccan government suddenly had more capital. Ambitious development projects were initiated and little thought was given to the possibility that phosphate prices would decline. Military expenditures also rose due to Morocco's absorbtion of the former colony of Spanish Sahara, which resulted in a guerrilla war with elements of the local population that favored independence. However, in the early 1980s, phosphate prices began their fall. The government turned to external borrowing and, by 1983, it began what was to become a long series of rescheduling with both commercial banks and official creditors. Adding to the deteriorating economic situation was the reemergence of political discontent, first, in the riots of 1981 and, later, in reports of a military conspiracy against King Hassan in January 1983.

Morocco's first rescheduling in 1983 was accompanied by the initiation of a structural adjustment program, implemented with the assistance of the World Bank. It was not peacefully accepted, as the austerity it inspired led to the riots of 1984. Much of the structural adjustment measures, however, took root. In January 1990, the result of this program is, as *Financial Times* reporter Francis Ghiles noted, "bringing of the country's foreign trade rules, state monopolies and agriculture into the second half of the 20th century."[12]

Morocco's economic restructuring has brought a reduction in the state budget deficit, which was cut from 12 percent of GDP in 1983 to around 4 percent in 1989.[13] Direct state control of the economy now accounts for roughly 20 percent of the total and in December 1989, and a privatization program was passed in the parliament to sell 119 state-owned corporations. Moreover, state subsidies for staple foods have fallen by nearly one-half during the same period.

In terms of exports, Morocco has made significant advances in diversification away from a dependency on phosphates. In 1980, phosphates accounted for 31.2 percent of total exports; by 1988 that percentage was down to 11.6 percent.[14] Morocco now exports clothes, processed fruit, vegetables, and fish. Furthermore, efforts have been made to develop downstream industries in the phosphate sector, including the production of phosphoric acid and fertilizers.

Morocco, unlike South Korea and Turkey, has a long distance to go before debt management becomes a secondary concern. Negotiations for a Brady Plan debt reduction of its $4 billion commercial bank debt began in 1989 and continued into 1990, resulting in an agreement in April. Under the new accord, Morocco's commercial bank debt was rescheduled with a reduced interest rate margin and partial rebate on interest payments made since the beginning of 1989. In a second phase, the commercial banks agreed to negotiate a three-year debt-reduction program that will include bond swaps and debt buybacks as well as new money contingent on Morocco obtaining an Extended Fund Facility from the IMF. Morocco reached an agreement with the IMF in June 1990, which provided the North African country with a $130-million standby facility. Additionally, in September 1990, Morocco rescheduled its debt with the Paris Club and received the most generous terms on stretching out payments of any country to date. This was due to Morocco's efforts at structural adjustment as well as the pro-Western role the Kingdom played in the Persian Gulf crisis. There was some concern that the higher oil prices related to the crisis and a loss of Kuwaiti assistance would derail the country's recent progress.

Morocco has also been able to obtain short-term commercial credit from

European banks. In late December 1989, the parastatal Moroccan Bank for Foreign Trade (Banque Moroccaine du Commerce Exterieur, BMCE) signed an agreement with Spain's Banco Exterior de Espana establishing a 1-billion peseta commercial credit line. The combination of structural adjustment assisted by the World Bank and IMF and a limited return to certain markets indicates that Morocco is evolving along the same path as Turkey and possibly the Little Dragons (although at a considerable distance back).

Morocco, like Turkey, South Korea, and many Latin countries, has had to contend with the issue of public opinion and a gradual liberalization of the political system. Although King Hassan continues to dominate the political landscape, fairly open parliamentary elections were held in September 1984, followed by provincial and prefectural elections in August. Since then, Parliament has played a more active role in the country's political life. In fact, in May 1990, a united front of opposition parties called for a vote of no confidence against the government over the budget. This was the first such action since 1964. Although the motion was easily defeated by the promonarchy parties, it indicated an opening in the country's political life. It may also indicate a future vocalization for greater political freedoms, especially as the structural adjustment process continues.

A FEW COMPARISONS

Tables 9.3 and 9.4 are meant to provide a better basis of comparison between South Korea, Turkey, and Morocco on the one hand and the three largest Latin American debtors, Argentina, Brazil, and Mexico on the other hand. It should be emphasized that these are at best rough indicators for comparison.

Although Latin countries have improved with their trade performance in the late 1980s, the three non-Latin countries made far greater strides, as reflected by Tables 9.3 and 9.4. It should also be remembered that Brazil in 1988 was the world's ninth largest economy and has a strong export orientation.

Table 9.5 reflects the capacity to pay. Turkey's external debt increase from 1987 to 1988 was a source of concern, but efforts were successfully made in 1989 to reduce debt-payment capacity to around 40 percent (it is difficult to estimate 1990's ratio due to the loss of export earnings from Iraq and higher oil prices). However, it should be noted that Turkey continues to have access to international capital markets, which only Mexico does of the three Latin countries (Chile and Venezuela also had access in 1990).

Although the capacity to handle external debt repayment is important, the rate of growth is also important. Table 9.6 provides an indication of the different real GDP growth rates among the countries.

Another area of comparison worth mentioning is inflation. Both Morocco and South Korea have inflation levels under 10 percent. Turkey's inflation was problematic in the late 1980s, rising to 74 percent in 1988, before falling to 68 percent in 1989. Inflation is estimated at 54 percent in 1990 by the Central Bank. Whereas

Table 9.3
Total External Debt
(in U.S. $ billions)

	1980	1982	1985	1987	1988	1989E
Argentina	27.2	43.6	51.0	58.4	58.9	59.6
Brazil	70.8	92.2	104.6	123.4	114.6	114.6
Mexico	57.4	86.0	96.9	109.3	101.6	95.9
Morocco	9.7	12.4	16.3	20.1	19.9	20.1
South Korea	29.5	37.3	47.2	40.5	37.2	33.7
Turkey	19.1	19.7	26.0	40.9	39.6	41.3

Sources: The World Bank, *World Debt Tables, 1989–90, First Supplement* (Washington, D.C.: The World Bank, 1990); and for South Korea in 1989, Republic of Korea Ministry of Finance estimate for January–September 1989; and for Turkey, Central Bank of Turkey estimate for the year (does not include foreign military debt).

Table 9.4
Total External Debt to Exports of Goods and Services
(in percentages)

	1980	1982	1985	1987	1988	1989E
Argentina	242	447	471	628	480	497
Brazil	304	393	341	417	305	304
Mexico	259	312	316	346	302	252
Morocco	224	327	364	328	283	287
South Kore	131	132	138	71	52	45
Turkey	332	196	188	244	201	192

Source: The World Bank, *World Debt Tables, Vol. 2, Country Surveys* (Washington, D.C.: The World Bank, 1990).

Table 9.5
Total Debt Service to Exports of Goods and Services
(in percentages)

	1980	1982	1985	1987	1988	1989E
Argentina	37.2	50.0	81.8	71.0	37.1	36.6
Brazil	63.1	81.3	42.2	37.0	47.0	31.9
Mexico	49.5	56.8	54.1	38.8	45.7	36.5
Morocco	32.7	43.2	27.0	25.6	24.3	30.0
South Korea	19.7	22.4	27.7	28.8	13.6	11.7
Turkey	28.0	29.5	31.8	32.9	40.6	34.7

Source: The World Bank, *World Debt Tables, Vol. 2, Country Surveys* (Washington, D.C.: The World Bank, 1990).

Table 9.6
Rate of Real GDP Growth
(in percentages)

	1980–1987
Argentina	−0.3
Brazil	3.3
Mexico	0.5
Morocco	3.2
South Korea	8.6
Turkey	5.7

Source: The World Bank, *World Development Report* (New York: Oxford University Press, 1990).

Mexico has made considerable progress in reducing its inflation from 159 percent in 1987 to 19.7 percent in 1989, Argentina ended the year at 4,923 percent, Peru at 2,775 percent, and Brazil at 1,765 percent.[15] In the Argentine case, in particular, this has been reflected in the "culture of inflation," which, according to William C. Smith, "led most Argentines, regardless of social class or eco-

Table 9.7
Emerging Stock Markets, 1989
(Market Capitalization in U.S. $ billions)

	1982	1985	1988	1989	1990 2nd qtr.
South Korea	4.4	7.4	94.2	141.0	110.3
Brazil	10.3	42.8	32.2	44.4	29.9
Mexico	1.7	3.8	13.8	22.6	29.9
Argentina	.974	2.0	2.0	4.2	3.2
Turkey	.952	–	1.1	6.8	15.8
Morocco	.292	.255	.446	.621	NA

Source: International Finance Corporation, *Emerging Stock Markets Handbook* (Washington, D.C.: International Finance Corporation, 1990).

nomic circumstances, to act on the expectation that inflation would either remain high or rise even more in the near-to-mid future.''[16] Although there are indeed other examples of hyperinflation and the development of a culture of inflation, as in Israel in the mid-1980s, it appears that it has been the most prevalent in Latin America in the 1980s.

The emerging differences between these countries is also reflected by a deepening in local financial systems. Although this should not be overstated, it is another element in the development process with repercussions for such areas as capital generation and a broadening of the base of national wealth. Tables 9.7 and 9.8 reflect this process. The first shows the development of emerging stock markets and the second, the number of "world class" banks as defined by Euromoney's "Top 500 Banks in the World."

It is worth noting emerging stock markets have continued to enjoy growth in 1989 and 1990. Turkey's market, the Istanbul Stock Exchange, although still small, grew rapidly through 1989 and 1990, reaching past the historic 5,000-point index barrier shortly before the Iraqi invasion of Kuwait on August 2, 1990. At the same time, many of these markets remain relatively shallow in terms of quality companies traded. The Moroccan bourse continues to lag behind due to the slowness of financial liberalization measures and the incremental movement of the country's privatization program. South Korea's stock market is also relatively new and many of the players in the market are learning that as the market goes up, it can also have a downward adjustment, as reflected by the downswing between 1989 and the second quarter of 1990.

Table 9.8
Number of Major Developing Country Banks
(Euromoney's Top 500; by Shareholders Equity)

	1984	1988
Argentina	3	1
Brazil	12	9
Mexico	3	1
South Korea	7	9
Turkey	3	4
Venezuela	2	0

Source: *Euromoney*, June 1985 and June 1989.

THE MARKET-ACCESS QUESTION

Have the developing countries that have made many of the economic reforms been rewarded by a return to the "voluntary" international capital markets? There are two important components to this answer. First and foremost, many of the non-Latin American countries that have undergone this process, with the exception of most of Sub-Saharan Africa, have found doors open to them. The second part of the answer is that although many Latin American countries have made reforms, like Chile, or have not rescheduled like Colombia, the return to the market has been greatly complicated by the contamination factor. Simply stated, many Latin American countries are in the wrong neighborhood and consequently are tainted with the same brush as problem cases like Argentina and Peru. The experience in the 1980s, therefore, was largely negative for Latin American borrowers. However, it is important to note that in 1990, Chile, Mexico, and Venezuela have found new credit options open to them, largely due to the reformist nature of their economies.

Tables 9.9 and 9.10 are derived from data supplied by *Euromoney* and can be regarded only as a rough indicator of market access. It should also be noted that in Table 9.9, $3 billion of the amount under Mexico's column came from a rescheduling agreement. At the same time, that was only syndication that was the result of a rescheduling. It should be added that since Mexico signed the Brady Plan accord, it has been able to borrow overseas again, bringing nearly $1 billion in 1990 in the form of bond issues for oil exploration, electric power plants, and modern telephone equipment.

Who was doing business in these countries?

Table 9.9
Market Access to Syndicated Loans, Feb. 1988-Dec. 1989
(in U.S. $ millions)

Country	Number of Syndications	Amount	Average in Years
Argentina	2	174.0	5.3
Brazil	3	117.5	2.3
Mexico	12*	3,646.5	2.8
Morocco	3	136.3	1.0
South Korea	23**	1,442.0	4.4
Turkey	52***	3,808.4	2.3

Source: Euromoney.
* Number includes three loans that equal 90 million British pounds.
**Number includes two loans equal to 9.7 billion yen and one loan for 16.9 million British pounds.
***Number includes two yen loans for 42 billion and a DM million loan.

To clarify Table 9.10 further, it should be noted that the lead banks often do not assume the complete exposure of the loan, but sell it off to other banks interested in acquiring assets. For many U.S. banks, the emphasis has been on generating fee income, not asset growth. This explains, in part, why U.S. banks lead in number of syndications in Turkey, but why actual U.S. commercial bank loan exposure has consistently fallen throughout the decade: in June 1982 it was $1.4 billion; in September 1989, it was $818 million.[17]

THE ECONOMIC AND POLITICAL
DEVELOPMENT QUESTION

One of the great riddles in development is what should come first—reforms that open the political system or reforms that open the economy. An understanding of this debate is critical for Latin America as well as other developing countries in the 1990s, especially in context to the external debt problem. It is often argued that the development track pursued by countries like South Korea, Singapore, and Morocco is nondemocratic and that ultimately lack of political liberties results in the downfall of the regime. However, it can be argued with equal validity that success in creating a more open political system does not always guarantee economic freedom as evidenced by the trials and tribulations of presidents Raul Alfonsin and Carlos Menem in Argentina. This is not meant to be a value judgment or a stated preference for authoritarian regimes over democracies, but

Table 9.10
Nationality of Lead Banks for Country Syndications
(Feb. 1988–Dec. 1990 includes colead)

	Number of Syndications	U.S.	Japan	Europe	Middle East	Other*
Argentina	2	2	–	–	–	–
Brazil	3	3	–	–	–	–
Mexico	12	3	1	8	–	–
Morocco	3	–	–	–	2	1
South Korea	23	8	13**	–	1	2
Turkey	52	29	16	16	13	2
Total	95	35	30	26	16	5

Source: *Euromoney*. *Includes Korean banks and the International Finance Corporation.
**Includes Morgan Grenfell Japan and Instituto Bancario San Paolo di Torino (Tokyo).

a fact that economic success can elude or be achieved by either political system, dependent on a number of variables, like interest rates, natural disasters or commodity prices.

Nondemocratic governments have an affinity to economic development policy that makes them appear more apt to be successful. Political scientist Carlos Miranda noted in a case study on Paraguay that there were four reasons why "authoritarian" regimes center their policy efforts on the economy: (1) "most such regimes comprise military officers who, at least in Latin America, have a solid technical education"; (2) "autocrats can exercise full control over the economic system without worrying about political implications"; (3) "economic policy receives attention in authoritarian regimes because of the reduced political expectations of the population"; and (4) economic policy is important to the life of an authoritarian regime because "when successful, it yields a sense of well-being and accomplishment—albeit false—to both the citizenry and the leadership."[18]

Miranda's points have considerable credence in the cases of Argentina in the 1970s and Brazil in the 1960s and 1970s. Chile under General Augusto Pinochet provides another example. Yet, it can be argued that failure on the economic front can be and has been a key factor in many such regimes, especially in the 1980s, when the external debt crisis greatly impinged on the ability of authoritarian governments to develop the promised "goodies."

Latin American nations are not the only nations that have grappled with the trade-offs between political and economic development. The Asian NEIs, especially South Korea, appear to have opted for economic development that includes an improved standard of living over political development. President Roh, in certain regards, is like General Pinochet: the Korean leader sees himself as the overseer of a political transition from military to civilian rule. The 1992 elections in South Korea could well be the country's most open and competitive. Roh has already stated that he will not run again and indicated that his main concerns are to gradually institutionalize democratic principles, while maintaining a framework of capitalism. In those respects, the Korean leader sounds much like Chile's President Aywlin or the two Argentine presidents since the end of military rule, Alfonsin and Menem. The comparisons extend further when examining the chief concerns of each leader being international competitiveness— for South Korea, how to maintain and improve the edge through high tech, and for many Latin American countries, how to get back into the game. Turkey's experience to some extent mirrors South Korea's, although efforts to establish a working democratic system predate the Second World War.

The attraction of economic progress for a nondemocratic or quasidemocratic government is also evident in Morocco. As Mark Tessler and John Entelis noted of the role of economic programs for King Hassan's rule: "Direct economic benefits are the most central element in Hassan's political calculus."[19] Although problems remain, such as with the distribution of national wealth, the overall standard of living has improved and politics at the beginning of the 1990s is more open. However, as Tessler and Entelis commented: "Despite the success of the 1984 elections, democracy is not present if it depends on the monarch's mood, on his calculations about whether liberalism or repression is the most effective way to contain challenges and maintain political supremacy."[20]

The cases of South Korea, Turkey, and Morocco offer different points of comparison to Latin America's development experience in terms of the interchange between political and economic factors. Ultimately, each country evolves in its own unique way, dependent on past experiences and cultural outlooks. In terms of the external debt problem, regime survival remains dependent on a societal understanding of the crisis and the ability of the government to present its programs as a plausible solution. Structural adjustment programs, with their longer-term nature and permanence, have been successful in countries like South Korea and Turkey primarily because people have understood why they must make sacrifices for the national benefit. For the majority of Latin American democracies in the 1990s, this will be a critical challenge.

CONCLUSION

It is understood that each country has a unique path to development and, hence, different ways in dealing with the issue of external debt management. However, a broad-based comparison does show something: for a number of countries, the movement to more open, trade-based economies can provide a growth model capable of resolving the external debt problem. In addition, in a very broad sense South Korea, Turkey, and Morocco shared certain factors that contributed to their relative successes: strong leadership and central control; a general, societywide consensus on reforms; a commitment to economic priority on the part of the state; staffing of the civil service with technocrats; a nurturing of the private sector; development of an export-based expansion; and, above all else, a flexibility of economic planning to changing circumstances. Despite the existence of authoritarian or near-authoritarian political systems in each case, South Korea and Turkey are pursuing democratic paths. Morocco's political system is perhaps best described as "democratic–evolutionary"—that is, evolving toward a more democratic system.

Latin America as a region at the beginning of the 1990s lags behind in making many of the necessary changes and runs the risk of becoming economically irrelevant in the international system. As Abraham Lowenthal noted in mid–1990: "Latin America's share of world commerce fell during the 1980s from about 6% to 3.5%. Its terms of trade worsened markedly, with a decline in the real value of almost all its commodity exports."[21] Moreover, the problems confronting Latin America will continue to be diminished in terms of importance on the global agendas of Washington, Moscow, Bonn, Paris, and Tokyo as long as rapidly changing events in Eastern Europe and the Middle East grab the headlines. Although a number of countries show considerable promise—Chile, Mexico, and Venezuela—some of the largest in terms of economic size— Argentina, Brazil, and Peru—continue to be whipsawed about by inflation and market changes.

South Korea and, over time, Turkey and Morocco demonstrate that the debt crisis has another side in which certain countries have not been dismal failures. The way forward for these countries, Turkey and Morocco more so than South Korea, is difficult, politically and socially painful, but in the end may provide a more solidly based future for the people of each country. Their respective development also opens the possibility of new markets for commercial banks, although in a more mutually cautious way than before and through innovative new products. However, before a Morocco or an Argentina returns to the international capital market in any significant capacity, the desire to make the necessary changes to repay past obligations must come from within each country; otherwise, outside assistance means little and the threat of reliving past mistakes becomes a reality.

NOTES

1. The World Bank's list of the nineteen most Severely Indebted Middle-Income Countries consists mainly of Latin American countries. Out of the nineteen listed, twelve are Latin American. The non-Latin American countries are The Congo, Cote d'Ivoire, Hungary, Morocco, Poland, and Senegal. See The World Bank, *World Debt Tables*

1989–90: External Debt of Developing Countries, Volume 1. Analysis and Summary Tables (Washington, D.C.: The World Bank, December 1989), p. 30.

2. John Williamson, *The Progress of Policy Reform in Latin America* (Washington, D.C.: Institute for International Economics, January 1990), p. 1.

3. See Bela Balassa and John Williamson, *Adjusting to Success: Balance of Payments Policy in East Asian NICs* (Washington, D.C.: Institute for International Economics, June 1987); Jon Woronoff, *Asia's 'Miracle' Economies* (Armonk, New York: M. E. Sharpe, Inc., 1986); and David Aikman, *Pacific Rim: Area of Change, Area of Opportunity* (Boston: Little, Brown, 1986).

4. Brian Kelly and Mark London, *The Four Little Dragons: Inside Korea, Taiwan, Hong Kong and Singapore at the Dawn of the Pacific Century* (New York: Simon and Schuster, 1989), pp. 18–19.

5. Ibid., p. 19. As Kelly and London noted: "For instance, tiny Singapore was heavily invested in Indonesia (population 170 million) and Malaysia (20 million). Many businesses in Thailand (60 million) are run from Hong Kong or Taiwan. Lagging farther behind were the politically driven Philippines (60 million) and Sri Lanka (20 million), both with enormous potential and vast cheap labor pools. Then, of course, there was China, with its billion people waking from a socialist slumber and looking about for guidance."

6. Woronoff, *Asia's 'Miracle' Economies*, p. 23.

7. Ibid., p. 228.

8. Louis Kraar, "The Tigers Behind Korea's Prowess," *Fortune Special Issue: Asia in the 1990s* (Fall 1989), p. 36.

9. The World Bank, *World Debt Tables, 1989–90, Volume 2. Country Tables* (Wastington, D.C.: The World Bank, 1990), p. 202.

10. These figures are from the Republic of Korea's Ministry of Finance and were released in December 1989.

11. Most of this data were compiled from Turkish sources during two visits in 1988 and 1989 to Ankara and Istanbul and further coverage through publications since those trips. The main sources of information were the Central Bank of Turkey, the State Planning Organization, and several commercial banks, such as Dişbank and Yapi Kredi Bank, as well as interviews with economists and financial professionals, like Üstun Sanver, Secretary of the Turkish Banks Association. See Central Bank of Turkey in collaboration with the State Planning Organization and the Undersecretariat of Treasury and Foreign Trade, *Turkey: Economic Developments, Policies and Prospects* (Ankara: The Central Bank of Turkey, April 1988); and Merih Celasun and Dani Rodrik, "Turkish Experience with Debt: Macroeconomic Policy and Performance," in Jeffery D. Sachs, editor, *Developing Country Debt and the World Economy* (Chicago: The University of Chicago Press, 1989), pp. 193–211.

12. Francis Ghiles, "Morocco's Royal Paraphernalia Line the Road to a Modern Economy," *The Financial Times*, January 19, 1990, p. 4.

13. Ibid.

14. International Monetary Fund, *International Financial Statistics 1989 Yearbook* (Washington, D.C.: International Monetary Fund, 1989), p. 519.

15. Richard Johns, "Mexico Inflation at 10-Year Low," *The Financial Times*, January 10, 1990, p. 6.

16. William C. Smith, "Democracy, Distributional Conflicts and Macroeconomic

Policymaking in Argentina, 1983–89,'' *Journal of Interamerican Studies and World Affairs*, Vol. 32, No. 2 (Summer 1990), p. 4.

17. Information from the Federal Financial Institutions Examination Council, *Country Exposure Lending Survey* (December 6, 1982 and January 10, 1990).

18. Carlos R. Miranda, *The Stroessner Era: Authoritarian Rule in Paraguay* (Boulder, Colorado: Westview Press, 1990), pp. 101–102.

19. Mark A. Tessler and John P. Entiles, ''Kingdom of Morocco,'' in David E. Long and Bernard Reich, editors, *The Government and Politics of the Middle East and North Africa* (Boulder, Colorado: Westview Press, 1986), p. 393.

20. Ibid.

21. Abraham F. Lowenthal, ''Latin America Enters the 1990s,'' *The Aspen Institute Quarterly*, Vol. 2, No. 3 (Summer 1990), p. 55.

Selected Bibliography

Balassa, Bela, Gerardo M. Beuno, Pedro-Pablo Kuczynshi, and Mario Henrique Simo-
    nesn, *Toward Renewed Economic Growth in Latin America* (Washington, D.C.:
    Institute for International Economics, 1986).

Calleo, David P., *The Imperious Economy* (Cambridge, MA.: Harvard University Press,
    1982).

Cohen, Benjamin J., *In Whose Interest?: International Banking and American Foreign
    Policy* (New Haven: Yale University Press, 1986).

de Soto, Hernando, *El otro sendero: la revolución informal* (Buenos Aires: Editorial
    Sudamericana, 1987).

Feinberg, Richard, *Debt and Democracy in Latin America* (Washington, D.C.: Overseas
    Development Council, 1989).

Goldberg, Ellen S., and Dan Haendel, *On Edge: International Banking Band Country
    Risk* (New York: Praeger, 1987).

Griffith-Jones, Stephany, and Osvaldo Sunkel, *Debt and Development Crises in Latin
    America: The End of an Illusion* (Oxford: Clarendon Press, 1986).

Harris, Nigel, *The End of the Third World: Newly Industrializing Countries and the
    Decline of an Ideology* (Harmondsworth, U.K.: Penguin Books, 1986).

Institute for International Finance, *Fostering Foreign Direct Investment in Latin America*
    (Washington, D.C.: Institute for International Finance, July 1990).

International Monetary Fund, *International Monetary Fund Annual Report, 1990* (Wash-
    ington, D.C.: International Monetary Fund, 1990).

Kaufman, Robert R., "Democratic and Authoritarian Responses to the Debt Issue: Ar-
    gentina, Brazil, Mexico," *International Organization*, Vol. 39, No. 3 (Summer
    1985).

Kuczynski, Pedro-Pablo, *Latin American Debt* (Baltimore: The Johns Hopkins University
    Press, 1988).

Lowenthal, Abraham F., "Latin America Enters the 1990s," *The Aspen Institute Quarterly*, Vol. 2, No. 3 (Summer 1990), pp. 53–62.

MacDonald, Scott B., Margie Lindsay, and David L. Crum, editors, *The Global Debt Crisis: Forecasting for the Future* (London: Pinter Publishers, 1990).

Manley, Michael, "Southern Needs," *Foreign Policy*, No. 80 (Fall 1990), pp. 40–51.

Nelson, Joan M., editor, *Economic Crisis and Policy Choice: The Politics of Adjustment in the Third World* (Princeton: Princeton University Press, 1990).

Pastor, Manuel, Jr., *The International Monetary Fund and Latin America: Economic Stabilization and Class Conflict* (Boulder, CO: Westview Press, 1987).

Petras, James F., *Latin America: Bankers, Generals and the Struggle for Social Justice* (Totowa, NJ: Rowman and Littlefield, 1986).

Sachs, Jeffery D., editor, *Developing Country Debt and the World Economy* (Chicago: The University of Chicago Press, 1989).

Scheman, L. Ronald, and Norman A. Bailey, "Putting Latin American Debt to Work: A Positive Role for the U.S.," *Journal of Interamerican Studies and World Affairs*, Vol. 31, No. 4 (Winter 1989), pp. 1–22.

Smith, William C., "Democracy, Distributional Conflicts and Macroeconomic Policymaking in Argentina, 1983–1989," *Journal of Interamerican Studies and World Affairs*, Vol. 32, No. 2 (Summer 1990), pp. 1–42.

Stallings, Barbara, "Latin American Debt: What Kind of Crisis?" *SAIS Review*, Vol. 3, No. 2 (Summer/Fall 1983), pp. 27–40.

Stallings, Barbara, and Robert Kaufman, editors, *Debt and Democracy in Latin America* (Boulder, Colorado: Westview Press, 1987).

Williamson, John, *The Progress of Policy Reform in Latin America* (Washington, D.C.: The Institute for International Economics, January 1990).

Woronoff, Jon, *Asia's "Miracle" Economies* (Armonk, N.Y.: M. E. Sharpe, Inc., 1986).

The World Bank, *World Bank Annual Report 1990* (Washington, D.C.: The World Bank, 1990).

The World Bank, *World Development Report 1990* (New York: Oxford University Press, 1990).

Index

About the Contributors

Uwe Bott is a German citizen. He works as a Senior Analyst with Moody's Investors Service, one of the largest rating agencies in the world. His responsibilities encompass soverign risk analysis of the countries of Central Europe. Prior to his current position, Mr. Bott held the position of Programming Officer with the Inter-American Development Bank, where he designed country programming papers, the Bank's medium-term investment strategies for its Latin American borrowing countries. He has published a number of articles on the economic and social development of Latin America. Mr. Bott, who holds a degree in law as well as in economics from the Albert-Ludwigs-Universitaet in Freiburg, Germany, was also a Fulbright Scholar at Georgetown University in Washington, D.C. Besides his native German, he speaks English, Spanish, and Portuguese.

Jane Hughes is an adjunct professor of economics at Brandeis University's Lemberg Program in International Economics and Finance. She also serves as a Senior Advisor to Political Risk Services, a division of IBA, USA, and consults with multinational corporations on international investment issues. She is the author of a major study on sovereign risk, and has published and lectured widely on international financial management. Before joining the Brandeis faculty, Ms. Hughes was a vice president with Manufacturers Hanover Trust Company in New York and Boston. She earned a bachelor's degree magna cum laude from Princeton University, a master's degree in international relations from the Johns Hopkins University School of Advanced International Studies, and an MBA from New York University.

Paul Luke is the Economic Adviser to Chartered West LB Limited in London. He has a B.Sc. in Economics, first class honors, from the University of Wales (1974) and a Post Graduate Diploma in Business Studies (1980). Between 1977 and 1986, he worked for the Bank of England, with a two-year secondment to the United Kingdom Cabinet Office (1982–1984). Between 1984 and 1986, he headed up the Latin American Group in the Bank of England's International Division. From 1986 to 1990, he was Assistant General Manager—Economics for Libra Bank, PLC. Mr. Luke has written extensively on various aspects of the United Kingdom's and international economics, including articles in *Economic Trends*, *Parliamentary Affairs*, *The Bank of England Quarterly Bulletin*, and *The Bulletin of Latin American Research*, as well as in the British and Latin American press. He has presented papers to the Institute of International Finance (in Washington, D.C.), the Society for Latin American Studies, the Research Unit on European–Latin American Relations, and to various universities. His most recent works include a contribution to G. Philip's (ed.) *The Mexican Economy* and an Economist Intelligence Unit publication (September 1989), *Venezuela to 1993—A Change in Direction?*.

Scott B. MacDonald is the International Economic Advisor at the Office of the Comptroller of the Currency in Washington, D.C. In that capacity, he handles the following issues: money laundering and monetary and macroeconomic developments in Western and Eastern Europe, the Middle East, and Latin America. Prior to that post in 1988, he was the Chief International Economist for Maryland National Bank and American Security Bank. He received his BA from Trinity College in Hartford, Connecticut, his MA in Area Studies from the University of London's School of Oriental and African Studies, and a Ph.D. in Political Science from the University of Connecticut. He has published in the *Journal of Inter-American Affairs and World Studies*, *Middle East Insight*, *The Times of the Americas*, and *Leaders*. His most recent books are *Dancing on a Volcano: The Latin American Drug Trade* (1988), *Mountain High, White Avalanche: Cocaine and Power in the Andean States and Panama* (1989), and a co-edited book, *The Global Debt Crisis* (1990). He has widely traveled in Latin America, especially in Brazil, Chile, Colombia, and Venezuela.

Allen M. Rodriguez is a Senior International Economist at the U.S. Treasury Department. He received an M.A. in Latin American Studies from Georgetown Univerity and his second M.A., this time in Economics, from the University of Maryland. From 1974–1977, Mr. Rodriguez was a Researcher at the World Bank in Washington, D.C., and from 1982 to 1983, he was a Senior Economist with the Bank of Montreal. From 1986–1989, he served as Financial Advisor to the U.S. Mission to the Organization for Economic Cooperation and Development (OECD) in Paris. Mr. Rodriguez plans to continue working on LDC debt and finance issues with the Treasury Department.

James Thornblade is a visiting professor of international economic relations at the Fletcher School of Law and Diplomacy of Tufts University. Previously, Dr. Thornblade held positions as economist, vice president, and senior international economist at the Bank of Boston from 1972 to 1990, where he directed country risk evaluation with an emphasis on Latin America and Asia. Prior to 1972, Dr. Thornblade was an instructor in economics at Syracuse University and economic analyst at the Pay Board, Executive Office of the President, Washington, D.C. He received a B.A. in economics from Oberlin College in 1963 and a Ph.D. in economics from the Massachusetts Institute of Technology in 1968. His publications include ''Textile Imports from Less-Developed Countries,'' in *Economic Development and Cultural Change*, articles in the *Boston Glode* and *Christian Science Monitor*, and numerous conference papers on international trade and country risk assessment. Dr. Thornblade has traveled extensively in Latin America.